THE STORY OF SURNAMES

By the same author

*The Middle Sea: A History of the
    Mediterranean*
The House of Wavell
The Stuarts of Traquair
The Story of Heraldry
Trace Your Ancestors
They Came With the Conqueror
The Golden Book of the Coronation
The Story of the Peerage
Tales of the British Aristocracy
Teach Yourself Heraldry and Genealogy
The Twilight of Monarchy
Princes of Wales
A Guide to Titles
The House of Constantine
Your Family Tree
*Ramshackledom: A Critical Appraisement
    of the Establishment*
*American Origins: A Handbook of
    Genealogical Sources Throughout Europe*
*Heraldry, Ancestry and Titles: Questions
    and Answers*
Heirs of the Conqueror

Books edited by the same author

Burke's Peerage, 1949–1959
*Burke's Landed Gentry (of Great Britain),
    1952*
*Burke's Distinguished Families of America,
    1939 and 1947*
Burke's Landed Gentry (of Ireland), 1958
*The International Year Book and
    Statesmen's Who's Who, 1953–1960*
*Author's and Writer's Who's Who, 1948
    and 1960*
Who's Who in Music, 1949
Who's Who in the Free Churches, 1951

The Story of
SURNAMES

L. G. PINE
B.A., F.S.A. scot., F.J.I., F.A.M.S.,
Barrister-at-Law

CHARLES E. TUTTLE CO. INC.
RUTLAND, VERMONT

Published in 1966 by
Charles E. Tuttle Co. Inc.
Rutland, Vermont U.S.A.
Printed in Great Britain by
Hazell Watson & Viney Ltd
Aylesbury, Bucks
First published by Country Life Ltd
London W.C.2
Second impression 1967

929.4
ρ

Library of Congress Card Number 66-26839

Contents

Preface

In 1952 Country Life Ltd. published my book, *The Story of Heraldry*, which, after it had passed through two editions, was published again in a third edition in 1963. The publishers then asked me to write a similar book, *The Story of Surnames*.

Here then is the result, and I should like to explain that this is not a dictionary of British surnames. Such dictionaries do exist, among the most notable being those by the late Canon Bardsley and by Dr Reaney. Rather I have attempted to explain the rules which govern the growth of surnames, and to encourage the reader to learn how to trace his own surname and its origin. Etymology is closely connected with genealogy when we treat of surnames, and thus the present book is in harmony with the works which I have produced on genealogy, heraldry, peerage and titles. In all cases I have tried, while doing my best to explain the subject, to get the reader, so to speak, to aim at working out his own salvation. When I first began the study of genealogy, with which that of surnames is so much linked, it was the impossibility of understanding the books suggested to me as guides which led me to teach myself the principles involved, and then to endeavour to pass on the results of my researches to others.

I do not claim for this book, therefore, that it is anything more than a guide, and certainly I do not view it in Horace's words as *monumentum aere perennius*. I shall be happy if it leads many more people to the fascinating study of their surname and their family. It has been a laborious work to produce, and I can now understand Cardinal Newman's remarks after the conclusion of his work on Justification; even more Pope's complaint that translating the Iliad was a task which lay on him day and night—so many lines a twenty-four hours, like a school imposition. Now I feel released, for a short while at least, until I turn to fresh woods and pastures new.   L. G. Pine

I. Introduction to the Subject

The ancient saying *ex Africa venit semper aliquid novi* could be varied for the New World, in the sense that ex America something old is always arriving. In my experience of thousands of genealogies, I have found the hoariest legends and the hardiest myths to circulate among my Transatlantic inquirers. Genealogy and the study of surnames are two subjects inextricably entwined; and from an American source comes one of the finest explanations of the origin of a surname which I have ever read. From an American of very respectable background and professional attainments, I received the story of the old Norman name Hamon or Hammond (surnames like most other words assume varying forms in traversing the centuries.). His thesis was briefly that the name Hamon stemmed from the ancient Egyptian god Amen Ra of Thebes, and therefore had seven millennia behind it. To this idea he had devoted an elaboration of some eighty type-written pages. Perhaps I need not add that this theory cannot be entertained by serious scholars. The name Hamo or Hamon is an old Norman name, which can quite genuinely be traced back for a thousand years into the Normandy which had been settled by the invading Norsemen or Vikings in the tenth century. In the course of ages this Christian name has given rise to the variants of Hammond, Hammand, Hammant, Hamman and Hammon. To add to the medley, Haim, Haimes, Haymes and Hamon all derive from the same source.

In contrast to the learned American, mentioned above, was a Canadian pilot who had the name of Mundy, which happens also to be the surname of a well-known Landed Gentry family. I was interested and asked him about his surname, to which he replied, varying the quotation: 'What's in a name? They can be changed when you like.'

Few people perhaps realise that surnames are of late origin, and that they can be changed as one pleases. Of surnames as such there were hardly any in the England of pre-Conquest days, if by surnames we mean our modern idea of a fixed name or mark by which a man is known. The last Saxon King of England—Harold II, who fell at Hastings—was called Harold Godwinson, as being the son of the great Earl Godwin. But this was to distinguish him from the many other Harolds of the time. Another notable Harold, who at the time of the Conquest was King of Norway, and whose mortal remains have long since dissolved into the good Yorkshire earth which our Saxon Harold allotted for him, was denominated Harold Hardrada, or Harold Hard Counsel. Yet another contemporary Harold was Harold Harefoot, a son of the great Canute. He was so called from his speed of foot.

Clearly then among the English and Danes of the immediate pre-Conquest time there were no surnames as we understand them. In France, however, surnames started about the year 1,000 A.D., and the first English writer to discourse on the subject says this, adding 'but not in England till about the time of the Conquest, or else a very little before, under King Edward the Confessor, who was all Frenchified.' Thus William Camden in his *Remaines concerning Britain*. In a work prepared by the late Lewis C. Loyd, entitled *The Origins of Some Anglo-Norman Families*, one will find plenty of evidence of the use of surnames among the Normans. Thus the well-known name Curson (Curzon) is traced back to a place called Notre-Dame-de-Courson, in Calvados, arr. Lisieux, cant. Livarot. Les Trois Minettes, again in Calvados, gave us De Tribus Minetis, which believe it or not was eventually Englished into Tremlett. Tracy was a Norman name, but it is not clear which of the places in Normandy called Tracy gave its name to the family which emigrated to England during Conquest days.

To assign an origin in Normandy for a surname is but to throw the question of its meaning and derivation further back. How came surnames to be used and what do they mean? To answer this question we must grasp three principles. First of all surnames are a rare possession among the nations of the world. In many countries the very name of the man is kept a secret, because to know it and use it might mean to gain power over him; so he goes through life with a nickname or secondary name, while his real name is known only to a select few. Even quite civilized nations often lack a surname in the modern European style. This is especially true of the countries of Asia and Africa.

In the present day surnames, like most other western inventions, have been exported and adopted, at least to some extent. Anyone, however, who has ever tried to compile an account of the former ruling Princes of India will know that surnames are much to seek in the Orient. Possibly they will now develop as in the west, but they still remain largely a European commodity. Nikita Kruschev shares the use of Christian or forename and surname with Lyndon Johnson and Harold Wilson (or Macmillan), whereas President Sukarno of Indonesia has only one name. A solitary instance in Europe of a single name is that of the great pianist, Solomon, as can be seen from his entry in *Who's Who*. In such cases a forename in all probability does duty as among our remoter ancestors for both that and a surname.

On the other hand, among the Romans the surname system soon reached clear and definite structure. A Roman normally had three names. There was the *praenomen*, which corresponded to our Christian or forename; this was followed by the clan or race name, and last of all came the *cognomen* or surname. Thus we have Marcus Tullius Cicero, or Gaius Julius Caesar, where the name by which the famous man is best known was his surname, but the name Julius is that of his *gens* or clan. His forename Gaius is seldom used except in formal accounts of his life. The Greeks had nothing corresponding to our surnames, but were content with the familiar 'son of' method of denoting their relationships.

During the period of the dark ages in western Europe, following the breakdown of the Roman empire, the Roman system of nomenclature was lost. It was only gradually during the later middle ages, from the thirteenth century onward, that surnames became steadily the civilised usage.

Surnames, then, are a rarity. When we come to question their meaning, we have to learn the meaning of place names, which have been very fruitful in creating surnames, and we must remember to link with the study of surnames that of genealogy. It may or may not be true, as Sir Harris Nicolas was quoted as saying, that most historical affairs had a genealogical side or meaning—but it is most certainly true that a false genealogy will give us a false meaning for surnames. The study of genealogy can and frequently does puff up a ridiculous family pride, but the true study of the subject makes for a much readier comprehension of history. Without genealogy who can understand the dynastic tables, which are a *sine qua non* of most historical periods before the rise of a qualified democracy? Without genealogy how can we know what was supposed to be happening in the Wars of the Roses, in the controversy between Stuart and Hanoverian, or in the mortal grapple of Elizabeth of England and Mary of Scotland? Similarly, unless we have studied genealogy or learned to absorb its ascertained results, we cannot get far with the study of surnames.

Surnames, it will be realised, are uncommon things in most of the world's history, and in our own country of England date only from the thirteenth-fourteenth century. In Wales they came much later, and their presence in Ireland and parts of Scotland requires very different criteria from those used in England. Surnames are derived in many cases from place names (the words of the Psalmist about calling the lands after their own names are not borne out by research, it usually being the other way round). Genealogical knowledge of the right kind will often enable us to decide the meaning of a surname.

Surnames fall into four classes. There are first of all the patronymics. Instances of these must occur to anyone. Robinson, Williamson, Robertson, Swainson, Johnson, Jones, Williams, Sims, MacMillan, O'Gowan, Thompson, Richardson—these are only a few of varying types, but all bearing clearly the sign of having come from the name of a father long past converted into dust and ashes, and probably more generations away than the ancestor of the fourteenth Mr Wilson.

Then come place names, of which there are an enormous quantity. Instances spring to mind—Olney, Churchill, Attlee, Home, Eden and Pine. Place names can be of two kinds. There are proper names such as Winchester, or London, or Bristol; there are place names in the most correct sense, but derived not from some named place, but from the characteristic of the ground. Thus Attlee is not a name of a place, but derived from some meadow, at the lee. Where was the lee which gave rise to the former Premier's surname? No one will ever know. The Attlee pedigree goes well into the eighteenth century, but then it is lost amidst a welter of Surrey Attlees, who rejoiced in identical Christian names and who lived in the same areas, thus making detection of the right line virtually impossible.

Occupation confers a multitude of names. Tailor (often disguised as Tailleur, and thought to be of French origin), Glover, Hunter, Butcher are instances. (Why is no one called Grocer?). Occupations early divide into two classes, owing to unfailing human snobbery. There are those names which belonged to a tradesman ancestor, such as those just mentioned. Then there are the names taken from offices—we might almost say professions. There are Priests and Priestleys galore (not by any means always derived from some medieval cleric who broke his vow of celibacy, but coming from such relatively harmless sources as the servant of a priest, or from a man who used to act a priest's part in the mystery plays). There is Chamberlain, not in most cases derived from any office of great profit or standing, but from the inn chamberlain, who looked after the arriving guests. The German name, now acclimatised in England, Zimmerman, brings it out better—room man, the fellow who allotted the guests their rooms in the inn.

Lastly we have nicknames, but most modern scholars are agreed that the area granted to these in discussing the meaning of names must be severely limited. For who would want to transmit to his descendants an opprobrious sobriquet? Many nicknames must have been given in the usual cruel human manner to people who in modern language are spastics, or mentally maladjusted; to cripples, in short, and to many such who would not be likely to have children. The habit of nickname-giving is a peculiarity of many branches of the human race. At its best it is most often a silly habit or a slovenly one, for what sense is there in altering a person's name; at its worst it is a symptom of the more vicious bent of the human mind. It is possible that in quite a number of cases a nickname has stuck. The great house of Scrope is considered to be Norman in origin and to have retained its Norse name, meaning 'crab', denoting possibly some long-forgotten ancestor's sidelong walk. Green (this may well be a place name, however), Brown, Strongitharm, Petit are other examples.

Yet there can be some colossal blunders in this section of surnames. Coward has got nothing to do with the timorousness of an ancestor; it is only cowherd. Deadman does not mean that some forbear was lacking in energy, but merely that he lived at Debenham in Suffolk. Godliman could denote, I suppose, a predecessor

13

in the sixteenth century renowned for his adherence to Puritanism, and the godly discipline of Master Calvin. It is much more likely to be a survival of the old spelling of Godalming in Surrey. Thus the nickname class is greatly reduced by the researches of modern scholars. Still, when we have a genuine nickname, it is a pity to darken counsel with learned explanations to prove that it is not one. Shakespeare is a plain and simple name—a spearman or user of a spear. The greatest authorities on surnames—Reaney, Bardsley, etc.—all concur in this explanation. To add to their testimony, if it were needed, one can state that when Shakespeare's grant of arms was rehearsed, reference was made by the Garter King of Arms (the notorious Dethick, who later went to prison for six months for false statements) to warlike forbears of the playwright.

Some names, of course, are on the fringe between nicknames and names of occupation. Alabaster is at first sight a curious surname. Does it refer to complexion? Was the original owner in a rudimentary cosmetic industry? No, his name is a corruption of arblaster or cross-bowman. Many names of this type must have come into the language in the time of the long French wars, from 1340 to 1453. The English from the time of Edward 1 (1272–1307) right on until the Tudor period developed the reputation for war which is normally given to the Germans. In that time they conquered Wales, held large parts of Scotland for long periods, gripped Ireland, in Professor Trevelyan's phrase, as a greyhound might hold on to a deer, conquered about one third of France, and restored a king to Spain. This considerable military achievement on the part of a people, who did not exceed more than four millions in that era, impressed foreigners and natives alike. Hence many surnames which might seem to be nicknames.

I have mentioned corruptions of names. This is a constant feature, not only of surnames but of words throughout the whole of English until the language began to harden. Right into the middle of the eighteenth century the language was still not crystallised, and it was probably not until after the publication of Dr Samuel Johnson's Dictionary that the final rounding off of English spelling could be said to have occurred. Even after that a writer like Sir Walter Scott a hundred and thirty years ago could write 'sate' where we would put 'sat'. Going back into the middle ages, we find many of our most familiar names spelt in half-a-dozen forms. Croindene is for our Croydon; Agmondisham for Amersham.

14

Even in one document a word could be spelt in more than one way. With surnames it was the same. We pronounce the name Raleigh as it is used in the place name in Devon. In Sir Walter Raleigh's own day, the pronunciation and the spelling was more often Rawley, as in James I's atrocious pun, 'I think but rawly of ye, mon.'

There was no fixity of surname among our ancestors. To us an *alias* may well denote something criminal or not quite nice, but this is a narrowed meaning unknown in the past. 'Your loving kinsman, Oliver Williams, alias Cromwell,' was the conclusion of a letter from the great Protector to his clerical relative, Archbishop Williams. And why not, for the real name of the Cromwell line was Williams, this name having been changed to Cromwell, at the suggestion of a formidable sponsor, Henry VIII, who extended to the new Cromwell, alias Williams, the patronage which he had given and later so drastically removed from the latter's uncle, Thomas Cromwell. In Keble's edition of Hooker's works, there is a short pedigree of that famous ecclesiastical writer's family. This shows us Hooker, alias Vowel, the well-known West country name which, in common with numerous other versions, comes from 'fowl', meaning a bird, and was used as a personal name and a nickname.

The familiar instance in *Tess of the D'Urbervilles*, in which Thomas Hardy showed so much genealogical skill, gives us a man called Stokes, who on buying some property in a part of England different from that in which he had made his fortune, began to think of changing his name. Having visited the British Museum and studied the county family histories, he came upon the name of D'urberville. 'He considered,' wrote Hardy, 'that D'urberville looked and sounded as well as any of them: and D'urberville accordingly was annexed to his own name for himself and his heirs eternally.' The family were known at first as Stoke-D'Urberville, but soon dropped the Stoke. It may be added that the pages of *Burke's Landed Gentry* and indeed of *Burke's Peerage* also contain very many examples of hyphenated names, whose true story is not dissimilar to that of the novel.

If we wish to understand fully the sparsity of surnames before a period of some six to seven hundred years ago, we could do no better than consider the fact that our royal family had no surname, at least of any certainty, until 1917, when the name of Windsor was adopted. Sir Bernard Burke in one of his most interesting works, *Reminiscences Ancestral and Anecdotal*, asked the question, 'What

15

is the surname of the children of Her Majesty Queen Victoria?' He answered with an adaptation of Horace's words to his patron, Maecenas. 'I feel persuaded that the Royal House of Saxe-Coburg —*atavis edita regisbus*—has no surname'. Sir Bernard assumed that the great Queen had taken, or that her children had taken, the style of the Prince Consort's family, and were scions of the House of Saxe-Coburg. This opinion has not found favour with subsequent genealogists. Sir Bernard added: 'When the adoption of surnames became general, the ancestors of that illustrious race were Kings, and needed no other designation than the Christian name added to the royal title.' If we leave out the Saxe-Coburg theory, the family of Queen Victoria was of German origin, and the same principles would apply to the Hanoverians as to the Saxe-Coburgs. No surname was needed for such an exalted family.

Looking over the various dynasties which occupied the English throne before the Hanoverians, we have first the royal house of Wessex which stemmed from Cerdic; they had no surname, as we have already seen. Nor did the Danish kings who reigned in England between Ethelred the Unready and Edward the Confessor. No more had the Normans. When William the Conqueror's great-grandson, Henry II, came to the throne, he too had no surname. But surely he was the first of the Plantagenets, although this surname was not bestowed upon the family until long after Henry II's time. It is said that his father had noticed a plant growing in the rocks, the *planta genista*, which he adopted as his badge or crest. Hence the name of the family, and if so this was an instance of a royal line taking its surname from a nickname or sobriquet.

With the dynasty which succeeded the Plantagenets, that of Tudor, we have a surname for the simple reason that (*pace* all the efforts of paid Tudor genealogists) this royal house was originally only a family of small Welsh gentry. True enough a grand and lofty pedigree appears in *Burke's Extinct Peerage*, but after all the disguises have been taken off, it appears that the founders of the Tudor family were stewards to the princes of North Wales, of whom Llewellyn was the last, in the time of King Edward I (1272–1307). Tudor was certainly at first only a Christian name. The story goes that when Henry Tudor, Earl of Pembroke, succeeded to the English throne as Henry VII, he sent a commission down into Wales to seek out his ancestry; the findings appear to have merited the modern tag, Top Secret.

16

It is interesting that the Tudors should originally have been stewards to the Welsh princes, for the dynasty which succeeded them on the English throne derived their surname from the office which they held of steward to the Scottish Kings. Marjorie, the daughter of Robert Bruce, married Walter, the 6th High Steward of Scotland, and gave birth to a son, Robert, who eventually in 1370 became the first Stewart King of Scotland, under the title of Robert II. The spelling Stuart came from France with Mary, Queen of Scots. Of course, when we speak of these personages of past ages being stewards to a monarch, it must be understood that they did not necessarily carry out the lesser or more menial duties of a steward. They held the menial-sounding office of steward, as Gibbon says, because in the medieval times the greatest nobles desired to possess domestic positions at court hitherto reserved for servants.

In the cases, then, of both Tudor and Stuart, a surname did belong to the royal house, because originally that house was not royal, and had therefore fallen into the fashion of adopting a surname. With the princes of the House of Hanover, no surname existed, any more than with the Saxe-Coburgs because from their beginnings they had been royal and did not need a surname.

The question of a surname for our royal family did, however, become acute during the 1914–18 war. While we were engaged in the struggle against Germany, our sovereign was in the embarrassing position of owning kinship with the leader of the country's enemies, the Kaiser, who was George V's cousin. Several members of the royal family possessed German names and titles. The King referred the matter of a surname to the College of Arms. After some fumbling and discussion very different from the clear-cut ruling of Sir Bernard Burke, the then Garter King of Arms, Sir Henry Burke (son of Sir Bernard) arrived at the same conclusion as his father. King George V then decided that henceforth the royal family should have a name, that of Windsor. He issued a Proclamation the purport of which was to declare 'that the Name of Windsor is to be borne by His Royal House and Family and Relinquishing the Use of All German Titles and Dignities. . . . We . . . have determined that henceforth Our House and Family shall be styled and known as the House and Family of Windsor.'

Windsor is certainly a very English name, and the millennium-old association of the place with English royalty gives a peculiar appropriateness to its adoption by our royal family. As Windsor is a very old place name in England, it is natural that there should exist several variants of it. As well as Windsor there are Wincer, Winser, Winsor and Windzer. In days when simple explanations were more in fashion, the name was thought to mean the winding shore, from the windings of the Thames at that point. According to a very learned scholar, Professor A. H. Smith, in his *Place Names and the Anglo-Saxon Settlement* (1956), Windsor means 'the slope or bank with a windlass,' for pulling up boats, etc.

The subsequent history of the royal surname is interesting and not out of place. With the granddaughter of George V, a Queen again graced the English throne, but before she succeeded, Queen Elizabeth II had been married to the Duke of Edinburgh. She was therefore, before her accession, H.R.H. Princess Elizabeth, Duchess of Edinburgh. Her surname would then be the same as that of her husband, which was Mountbatten, the English equivalent of Battenberg, one of those names and titles renounced by members of the royal house in 1917 at the request of George V. After her accession to the throne, it would be possible for pedants to argue that the royal house had become the House of Mountbatten. On 9th April, 1952, two months after her accession, the Queen made the declaration in Council that it was her will and pleasure that she and her descendants, other than female descendants who marry, and their descendants, should bear the name of Windsor.

The surname of the Duke of Edinburgh on his naturalisation, six months before his marriage to the Queen in 1947, was that of his uncle, Earl Mountbatten. Previous to this naturalisation (which always carried with it the renunciation of previous titles), the Duke had been a Prince of the royal house of Greece and of Denmark (from which the Greek royal line is derived). His surname then was Schleswig-Holstein-Sonderburg-Glucksberg.

The tale of the Windsor surname is still not yet complete. In 1960, on 8th February, eight years after her accession to the throne, the Queen again made a declaration in Council concerning her surname. This declaration is so interesting that it deserves to be quoted in full:

'Whereas on the 9th day of April, 1952, I did declare in Council My Will and Pleasure that I and My children shall be styled and known as of the House and Family of Windsor, and that my descendants, other than female descendants who marry and their descendants, shall bear the name of Windsor. And whereas I have given

further consideration to the position of those of My descendants
who will enjoy neither the style, title or attribute of Royal Highness,
nor the titular dignity of Prince, and for whom therefore a surname
will be necessary: And whereas I have concluded that the Declaration made by Me on the 9th day of April, 1952, should be varied in
its application to such persons: Now therefore I declare My Will
and Pleasure that, while I and My children shall continue to be
styled and known as the House and Family of Windsor, My descendants other than descendants enjoying the style, title or attribute of Royal Highness and the titular dignity of Prince or Princess
and female descendants who marry and their descendants shall
bear the name of Mountbatten-Windsor.'

The Queen was certainly looking well ahead. This declaration
could apply only to the grandchildren of the present Prince of
Wales, apart from the eldest grandson, and of the Queen's subsequent other sons. Under a ruling of George V, the title and style of
Prince and Princess was restricted to his grandchildren. Hence the
possibility of the arrival in the royal family within three or four
generations of Mr and Miss Windsor. Now for the first time in
English history, a hyphenated surname will be borne by royalty.
Such surnames began to come into England during the eighteenth
century, when the joining of property became more and more important; and in order to prevent the disappearance of a once famous
name, it was often made a condition of inheritance or marriage that
two surnames should be used. Not only two but sometimes three
or even four, which must make social intercourse somewhat hard
at times. Will you have a cup of tea, Mr Walker-Cathcart-Heneage?
Could you move up, please, Mr Cameron-Ramsay-Fairfax-Lucy?
It must be a great relief to get on to Christian name terms.

If the first family in the British Commonwealth had no surname
until it decided to adopt one, then clearly any idea of a permanency
in surnames is a delusion. What, however, of changes of name to
which reference has been made above? What must we do if we wish
to change our surnames? Are we bound by law to go through complicated and expensive procedures? The answer is plainly and
simply, No. It is a principle of the common law of England that a
man may take what name he pleases, provided always that he has
no fraudulent purpose in so doing, and has no intention to inflict
a loss upon someone else. If, therefore, you feel that your merits are
being hidden by the name of Smith which you have inherited,

19

there is nothing to prevent you deciding one morning to face the world anew with Trefusis or even Plantaganet as your surname. Curious to relate, there is nothing to prevent the adoption of Windsor as your name. In republican France, the taking of the name of one of the great families of France is not permissible. Capet-Bourbon is out of the question, as an adopted name.

To change your name all that you need to do—is to change it. If you are called Godley and feel that Lust or Lusty is more fitting, then you can start the week next Monday as Lusty. To put it in lawyerlike language, your new name can be acquired by use and reputation. Any other change or form of change will merely be evidence that the change has been effected. So if you do not think Brown sufficiently distinguished, why not Cholmondeley-Marjoribanks, when you will have the additional pleasure of giving your acquaintances the difficulty of learning to use a peculiar pronunciation in support of the new names.

Cases in English law give us instances of changes as outstanding as from Abraham Langley to George Smith. The latter was the name in which the bearer got married, and it was held that the marriage was valid. In this case, and in many others, it will be observed that not only the surname was changed but the Christian name also. Strictly speaking, a Christian name cannot be changed since it is given in baptism; according to one of our learned judges in a case in 1946, a Christian name can be changed only by (i) an Act of Parliament, (ii) by a bishop at confirmation or (iii) by the addition of a name on adoption. While I think this to be correct, none-the-less Christian names are often changed, no doubt due to the lessening in religious faith which is one of the marks of modern England. As so many persons in the country have either ceased to be Christians or never held that faith, the use of the term forename has come widely into documents, such as official forms, and the change of the first name or names is now quite frequent.

However, despite the freedom with which the surname may be changed, it is advisable from many points of view that due attention should be drawn to the change. It is, therefore, a good idea to insert in the local newspaper a notice about the alteration, or if you prefer it, in *The Times*. The personal column of *The Times* is read by many who do not buy the newspaper, and a notice inserted therein is sure to gain the right amount of attention.

Supposing that you wish to register the new name and to have evidence of its change at the same time, then the best course is to make the alteration by deed poll. The deed poll must be made before a Commissioner for Oaths, commonly a solicitor. The declaration sets out that the person concerned does purpose to renounce absolutely the use of the former surname, and to use at all times thereafter the new name, as well for himself as for his wife and children. In the case of a married woman the consent of the husband is needed. The deed poll may be enrolled in the Filing Department of the Central Office of the Supreme Court. The charge for this is £2, and an added fee of one shilling for folios of 72 words which are contained in the deed. There is a stamp duty of ten shillings on the deed, and a filing fee of ten shillings is also payable with regard to the statutory declaration. The deed poll has to be advertised in the *London Gazette*. The copies of the enrolled deeds are kept at the Filing Department of the Public Record Office, Chancery Lane, London, W.C.2. The search fee is 2s. 6d. A deed poll change of name can be registered at the College of Arms in Queen Victoria Street, London, at a fee of fifteen guineas.

It should be observed that an alien cannot change his surname unless he has obtained exemption from the provisions of the 1919 Aliens Restriction Amendment Act. This prohibited the taking of another name by an alien other than that by which he was known on 4th August, 1914. This did not apply to a change by royal licence (see below) or to a name taken by a married woman on her marriage, this being her husband's name.

Many changes of name recorded in the *London Gazette* do apply to persons who were formerly aliens, but who have taken British nationality. I often think that some very unfortunate incidents will occur in some eighty or a hundred years' time, when a struggling genealogist has acquired a wealthy patron and begun work on the family tree of Cromwell or Howard, Grosvenor or Mountain, only to discover in the pages of the *Gazette* that in the years immediately after World War II, the original name had been Kwicienski, or Kratzoff, or Bergstein. The British refusal to limit the alien's choice of a surname is responsible for the apparent alliance of some mid-European native with one of the most noble houses of England or Scotland.

A much more expensive form of name change is that by royal licence. This is a change made and enrolled with the College of Arms. The fee for a royal licence is £54 13s. 10d. Nor is this the end of the bill, for other fees are payable to the College for the grant or exemplification of the coat of arms which always accompanies this form of name change. Indeed, a change under this method is almost always the result of a clause in a will whereby the beneficiary under the will is required to change his name and arms or to take additional name and arms to satisfy the wishes of the testator. The royal licence is given under the royal sign manual, since the grant or addition of arms must come under the jurisdiction of the sovereign. This type of change must go through the College of Arms not only because it involves the bearing of arms, which is under the aegis of the College, but also because the Courts, in construing the names and arms clauses, must have evidence that in fact the name and arms have been taken. A fair-sized body of legal cases exists on this aspect of the law, from which it emerges that (i) a name taken must be taken in perpetuity and if not persisted in would have the effect of divesting the user of the property to which he has succeeded under the will; (ii) a name and arms clause can be void for uncertainty in the wording, this being the tenour of *In re Murray* (1955), where an apparent conflict took place between two clauses of the will; and (iii) an objection can be taken to a name and arms clause on the grounds of public policy, an obligation being sometimes placed on a married woman to take a surname different from her husband's. Instances abound of names and arms clauses which have been implemented, in the pages of the *Peerage* or *Landed Gentry*. Their origin dates back about two hundred years and is the result of the property building habits of the British aristocracy. Some very curious surnames have resulted, such as Cave-Brown-Cave, or Plunkett-Ernle-Erle-Drax.

One of the peculiarities attending upon the hyphenation or addition of names is that in course of ages, after perhaps three or four wills, which have directed the beneficiary to take a name in addition to, or in substitution of, his own, someone comes to represent an ancient family who has no blood connection at all with those whose name he bears. An instance of this sort of thing occurred at the close of the Carey or Carew history in Beddington in Surrey. Cary or Carey (Carew is a variant) is a place name found all over the British Isles, being probably Celtic or aboriginal in origin. The famous family of the Careys of Devon took their name from a place of this name in the west country. One of their branches was settled at Beddington for over five hundred years, but in the end the last person to bear the name of Carew at Beddington was, fortunately for the family's fame, no blood relation, though he had succeeded under the usual testamentary dispositions and taken the surname. He was a spendthrift who in the early nineteenth century ran up debts to the sum of £350,000. To meet some of his liabilities he put a bet of £20,000 on a horse running in the Derby. The horse did not win, the gambler was made bankrupt (this must have been for his other debts, since a gambling or gaming debt cannot be prosecuted). The old manor house now belongs to the L.C.C. The details of the succession are given in the excellent parish *History of Beddington*, by the Rev. Thomas Bentham.

Similar instances of the use of surnames of great families can be found in the narratives in *Burke's Peerage* or the *Landed Gentry*. In the case of the Earls of Lytton, we have the surname of the family as Lytton, a place name in Derbyshire. This family flourished during the middle ages, until it died out in the male line with Sir William Lytton, who died without issue in 1704. He was succeeded by his great-nephew, Lytton Strode, who took the name of Lytton, but left the estates to his cousin on his mother's side, and so eventually the property and the surname passed through the families of Robinson, Robinson-Lytton and Lytton, with the famous novelist Bulwer-Lytton thrown in for extra measure.

A change of name can also be made by a very costly method, through a special Act of Parliament. This involves, of course, a private Act which must be promoted and presented. It has been said that the only thing which Parliament cannot do is to change a man into a woman or vice versa. It follows, then, that a change of surname by the promotion of a private Bill can change the whole of the names, Christian and surname alike.

With regard to the surnames of married women, the usual course has been and is to take the husband's name. There is no compulsion in the matter, and there have been occasional instances of a woman retaining her own maiden surname after marriage. There are more numerous examples of a man taking his wife's surname. This is not always due to excessive feminism on the wife's part, but to a variation of the old names and arms clause, by which the husband of an heiress may well be required to assume her name. The idea here is to give continuity to the ownership of the property and to preserve an historic name. Many are the instances hidden under the thick branches of a family tree, in

23

which a man's name has been sacrificed in order that the family themselves, and future ages also, may be deluded into assuming that the male line identity has been kept up from a remote period.

Nowhere is this more cleverly brought about than in the Percy family of Northumberland. They are not Percies at all in the male line. Not only was the iron-master, Smithson, called upon to sacrifice his own surname and arms for that of Percy, so that all trace of the Smithson arms has disappeared (or never did appear) in the Northumberland achievement, but several centuries earlier, when the heiress of Percy married Josceline de Louvain, he also became a Percy. The name Percy is another of those derived from a place in Normandy and is genuinely a surname brought over from that country at the time of the Conquest. Perhaps, then, it can be understood that the family were anxious to maintain their connection with so remote an origin.

What has always seemed strange to me, however, was the assumption by the grandson of the great Robert Clive of India, the 2nd Earl of Powis, of the surname of Herbert in lieu of his patronymic, Clive. Thus the name of Clive no longer appears among the lists of peerage surnames, and this not because the male line has been extinguished, but because the male surname has been substituted for another. Clive is, by the way, a place name of the second class, meaning much the same as 'cliff' or 'slope'; Herbert was introduced by the Normans, and can be construed as 'army-bright'. It has given rise to numerous forms, of which may be mentioned, in addition to Herbert, Herbit, Harbard, Harberd, Harbert, Harbird, Harbord, Harbot, Harbutt, etc.

Under the process of adoption a change of name may be made. Here the change is usually effected for an infant or minor.

An alteration of name made *bona fide* is effective for all purposes in English law. It is somewhat amusing to notice that while English law will not protect the most august surname from being taken by someone other than the former bearer of it, the law does extend its protection to the use of a name exclusively for trade. Here we come upon the principle that gain is sacred and must be upheld at all costs. It is similar with the use of coats of arms. Until quite recently (when the Court of Chivalry was formally revived) there was no protection for a coat of arms; a person named Howard, who fancied a nice decoration for his car or cuff-links, could adopt the arms of the Earl Marshal, the Duke of Norfolk, provided that he kept away from the supporters of the arms (to use these would be tantamount to personating the Duke) and nothing could be done to him in law, though the Duke of Norfolk is the head of the College of Arms. A trade mark, however, has been brought under the shield of law and given its support and protection.

We see, then, that there is nothing of a permanent or exclusive nature about surnames. For one great name which has persisted down the centuries, there are many, many more which have been altered and altered again, and which have passed through numerous changes. Some years ago I was interested in trying to trace the meaning of the name, Beswetherick, which is of Cornish origin and which I eventually ran to earth, to discover that it meant (in Cornish) 'the house by the meadow', meaning that the first bearer had lived in such an abode. A genealogist, who knew a good deal about Cornish families, told me that the name was traceable to the reign of Henry VI, when he thought that it had been changed from Williams. If this is the case, then the alteration was made without benefit of any deed poll or royal licence, by simple assumption.

In the course of succeeding chapters I shall analyse English surnames, but also give special attention to the surnames of Wales, Scotland and Ireland, and as far as possible (in this country) of Jewish names. There are some 100,000 surnames known in the British Isles, of which perhaps 25,000 have a genuinely proven meaning. In this book, I do not purpose to explain every name (not even of the 25,000), but to give guiding lines with ample illustration which will enable the reader to follow up the fascinating study of the meaning of surnames, his own being, of course, the most important.

Note. Those who would like to study further the legal aspect of the change of surnames would do well to read the booklet issed by the Solicitor's Law Stationery Society Ltd., namely *Change of Name*, by J. F. Josling, seventh edition, 1962. This gives much valuable information.

II. Norman Surnames

In any study which touches upon English genealogy it is as well to lay at the very beginning the ghost of the old legend, or rather myth, that such and such a family is of Norman descent. Of course, in view of the spreading of the Norman invaders all over England, and the fact that, far from being driven out, they were able to consolidate their hold and go on entering the country for close on two hundred years, it is not a matter of surprise to reflect that most of us have Norman blood. The Normans were ultimately absorbed into the English people, whom they had so cruelly outraged. They have disappeared except for the disagreeable habit of some of those, who are known as our best people, of describing themselves as Norman. The possession of a Norman name does not imply Norman descent, for as I have indicated, the fixity of surnames is a comparatively modern idea, and not too relevant even now. However, it is as well to know what are the Norman names, because the Normans were the first in England to use surnames.

Right in the front, as it were inviting comment, is the curious surname of D'Aeth. This has a Norman or French look about it, though it is really a refined spelling of Death. Dr Reaney remarks of this surname that it is just possible that it is derived from Ath in Belgium, but that most instances connect the name with the plain English word death. The origin would then probably be derived from a part in one of the old mystery plays. This is incidentally considered to be the origin of some otherwise very equivocal surnames, such as Priest, King or Pope. In the old mystery plays, such as the Wakefield Cycle, many characters occur of either Scriptural or moralistic nature, and there must have been instances where local people were as skilled in acting as are those who nowadays participate in the Oberammergau Passion Play. In older times, it would not be unnatural for the friends and neighbours to bestow a sobriquet upon a man for his ability in playing a part. Fortunately, we do not trace anyone called God, though in the mysteries an actor would have taken the part of God the Father.

Another interesting explanation of D'Aeth is that it is taken from a mercifully abbreviated form of God's death—'sdeath. The latter was employed in an attempt to avoid profanity. Strange to relate, in the church-enfolded society of the middle ages, many forms of impious oaths prevailed, which we have lost, but which have left their mark upon the surnames of our land. Dr Bardsley points out the variety of religious oaths, if such they may be termed, which spring out of the pages of the *Canterbury Tales*—e.g. Christ's passion, God's soul, God's dignity. Henry II used to swear by God's legs (just how he arrived at this particular form of blasphemy would perhaps tax a pyschologist to explain). Henry VIII liked to refer to God's body, meaning the Holy Sacrament. Some religious persons think that familiarity in daily life led these practitioners of religion to use such profane swearing. No doubt many more examples could be gleaned from the works of the industrious Dr Coulton, and even possibly one of those ingenious explanations of his, but the main point is that this form of objuration has left the legacy of a host of surnames—Pardew (Par Dieu), Pardoes, Bigod (the name of a great medieval family), Godbeare (now Godber), Wardieu, Goodspeed (from Godspeed), and possibly Blood from God's blood, abbreviated to 'sblood.

Enough in the way of requiem for D'Aeth.

Turning the pages of any modern work on Norman ancestry, we come upon many real Norman names, truly derived from some place in Normandy and brought here by the followers of the Conqueror or his descendants. Abernon is an example from Calvados. It should be noted that the 'de' of some English families is a slightly affected addition, since it is derived solely from the habit of the medieval scribe of writing down someone as being John or Thomas de London, or de Stokes, etc. The 'de' does not then necessarily denote any kind of lordship, as it might do on the Continent, where the French 'de' and the German 'von' denote at least a minor nobility.

It is also a matter of great interest in England that whereas lands usually bestowed rather than obtained a name, in some parts of England the newcomers from France succeeded in adding their surname to the places where they settled. This is particularly the case in the west country, as can be seen in Curry Mallet, Shepton Mallet, Hatch Beauchamp, Norton Fitzpaine, Stoke Courcy, Washbourne Pyne, Upton Pyne, etc.; but instances occur outside the confines of Devon and Somerset. Iron Acton, Stoke Mandeville, Stoke D'Abernon are examples from different counties of England. Aubigny, often found in the Italianate style of Albini, is another case of cross Channel derivation. So is Aumale, which gave rise to Albemarle. Bachepuis was the father of Bagpuize, as in Kingston Bagpuize. Bacon is another, and one can only ponder in some admiration at the huge number of persons whose surname is taken from an obscure place in northern France—Molay Bacon, in Calvados—and who must often have puzzled over the connection of their forbears with this common article of food. A Norman is named in the *Book of Fees*, who held one quarter of Bradford juxta Mare in Essex (where there is now an atomic power station). His name was William Bacon.

Baillieu or Bailleul derives from a place in the Seine Inférieure. The family of Balliol, who gave kings to Scotland and the name to one of Oxford's most celebrated colleges, came from Bailleul, dept. Somme, arr. Abbeville, cant. Hallencourt. As we shall see later when we deal with Scottish surnames, many Norman families went to Scotland, or branches of Norman families went from England, in the twelfth century, and thus some old Norman names became established in that country. Basset was a surname brought into England in Norman times, when Richard Basset is recorded as having come from Montreuil-au-Houlme, Orne. The meaning of the name is probably 'a person of low stature or low origin' and this agrees with some remarks of the twelfth-century historian, Ordericus Vitalis, that Henry II raised one of the Bassets from the dust to an exalted place.

A very widespread modern English name is that of Beaumont. Whatever may be thought of the ancestral aspirations of any living Beaumont, it is historically correct that Roger de Beaumont, who held Sturminster Marshal in Dorset, was from Beaumont-le-Roger, in Eure. Berners is from Bernieres-sur-Mer, Calvados. Calvados, whose modern renown is in apple-brandy, was also the home of a notable English (originally, of course, Norman) lord, Bigot or Bigod, who held a small fief in the department of Calvados. Bisset, which means dark in Old French, was the name of a family hailing from Cany in Seine Inférieure. Henry II had a steward who was named Manasser Biset, who married the heiress of the lord of Cany. The original seat or holding of the family of Biset or Bisset may have been in the Pays de Caux.

A famous name in medieval times is that of Bohun, once one of the greatest in England, now extinct in this form. Many readers will recollect the name of Bohun as being borne by a knight who, before the battle of Bannockburn, thought to end the long strife of England and Scotland by riding down King Robert the Bruce, only to have his helmet and head cleft in two by Bruce's battleaxe. The family was later to disappear as completely as the victim of the Scottish king. According to some, the modern Bone represents the medieval Bohun. In fact Bone is simply the anglicised form of Le Bon, and the Bones, Bonns, Bonnes and Bunns all get their surname from a person or persons who received the sobriquet of Bon, either for their natural goodness or for their handsome appearance or comeliness. So the Bones can be happy in knowing that their surname is numbered in the large class of names of French origin, but not among those of Norman barons.

The De Bosco family came from Normandy to hold lands in England. The name was Englished into Bois, and may be the ancestor of some of the numerous variants —Boyes, Boys, Boice, Boyse and Boyce. On the other hand, as the meaning of the word is 'wood', it must be obvious that many lines of families with a variant of this name would occur, since the person who lived near a wood might well be called Bois, if he were of French origin (if English in origin, Atwood is a good source). Still there was a notable French family who derived their name from Bois-Arnault, Eure.

The Boswalls, or Boswells, derive from Bosville, Boesevilla or Beuzeville-la-Giffard, in Seine Inférieure. Bussy or Bussey originate from De Buceio or Boceio, in Orne. The not very attractive name of Bully or Bulley was once that of a Norman family stemming from Bully in Seine Inférieure. Cailly is a direct importation, so is the name Cantelupe, which is at least still found in the peerage as a minor title of Earl de la Warr. Carteret is still the spelling of the place whence came this family close on nine centuries ago. Champernowne is from *De Campo Arnulfi*. Spelling has, of course, varied, being given as Cambernon, arr. and cant. Coutances.

The fine old name of Chandos is fron Candos, Eure. This great surname, which glittered across the battlefields of the middle ages, and still finds its lustre in the British peerage, is purely French.

Sir John Chandos, the friend of the Black Prince, who lost his life in the marshes around Bordeaux, was of French descent, yet he was the Flower of English Chivalry. The Chaworths came from de Cadurcis, de Chaorciis, namely Sourches in Sarthe. Chesney is from Le Quesnay in Seine Inférieure. Chesney has many variants—Cheyney, Cheyne (the reminiscence is to the Roland Cheyne of Sir Walter Scott's *Antiquary*), Chainey, Chaney, Cheeney, Chene, Cheney, Chasney, Chasteney, Chastney, Chesnay and Chestney, as well as to Chesney. According to Dr Reaney, all stem from the Middle French *casnetum*, which in Old French is *chesnai* or oak grove. The Cleres were from Cleres, and this name can also be a form of Clare, which is derived from Clare in Suffolk.

Coleville or Colville seems an English enough name, yet it has become so only after several centuries of anglicisation. It is derived from Colleville in Normandy. Corcelle or Curcella does, on the other hand, have the Frenchified air which Camden referred to. It is indeed of French stock all through, and comes from Courseulles-sur-Mer, Calvados. Yet there are those who derive the house of Churchill, which twice in Britain's darkest hour has given transcendently great leaders to our country, from the Seigneurs de Courcelle. In fact, Churchill is what the name implies— Churchill, a place in Somerset, or else a dweller near the church on the hill.

In his fine life of his ancestor, the first Duke of Marlborough, Sir Winston Churchill remarked that the original Sir Winston Churchill had traced his Lyon rampant argent upon a sable coat to Otho de Leon, Castellan of Gisor, one of whose youngest sons came into England with William the Conqueror. On which the great Prime Minister remarked dryly: 'All this was very fine, but when descending these chains we come to John, ancestor of the present Churchills of Muston, and Roger, who by the daughter of Peverell, relict of Nicholas Meggs, has issue Matthew, father of Jaspar, my grandfather, we enter a rather shady phase. Edward Harley rudely asserts "that John Churchill's great-grandfather was a blacksmith who worked in the family of the Meggs" and certainly as his great-great-great-grandfather married a Miss Meggs, this seems very suspicious and even disquieting.' Thus the twentieth-century Sir Winston in *Marlborough, His Life and Times* (1947, Book I, pages 33–34). He adds: 'In any case there are strong grounds for believing that John's grandfather solidly improved the fortunes of this branch of the Churchill family. He was a practising lawyer, a deputy registrar of Chancery as well as a member of the Middle Temple and lawyers were a prosperous class at this date. Not only did he make a marriage himself into an aristocratic family, the Winstones, but he seems to have arranged a step for his eldest son. For all the genealogical table produced by Winston, the Drakes were a more renowned and substantial family than the Churchills, of whom there were numerous branches of various conditions, some quite lowly, in Dorset alone.' So we see that only rigorous research can guarantee that your name is of Norman origin. I said as much as the great Sir Winston himself of his ancestry in my book, *They Came with the Conqueror*. 'Even the most legend-loving writers have given up the Seigneurs de Churchill!'

In the lists of Normanity many must be unhorsed who had previously thought of themselves as of the gentle Norman blood. As usually happens in human affairs, conversely there are many people who perhaps do not greatly concern themselves with these matters, who are of Norman origin. The name Costentin has passed through many forms, of which one, Constantine, has survived to this day. It may be derived from Coutances, or as Loyd suggested, from the Cotentin. It is certainly Norman. One need not be surprised at the source of Cressy. It seems, however, peculiarly appropriate that Cressy should be of French origin, considering that it was at Cressy or Crécy that for the first time after the Conquest (except perhaps for Tenchebrai) the French had a signal defeat on their soil from the English.

Curcy or Courcy is another instance of the transplantation of a name from across the Channel. Stogursey or Stoke Courcy, so famous through Bernard Shaw's mention of it in *St Joan*, derived its second name from the Courcy family, which settled there in Somerset. Their origin was from Courcy, Calvados. The noble family of the Lords Kingsale trace their descent from the Norman line of Somerset. Then, too, there is the great house of Curzon, of which Viscount Scarsdale is the present head. Their home over eight hundred years ago was at Notre-Dame-de-Courson in Normandy. The surname of Dunsterville is from Dunstanville, which in its French original was Denestanville, in Seine Inférieure. A very illustrious name is that of Ferrers, formerly the Earls of Derby (the name of the present Earl Ferrers is Shirley), which came from Ferrieres-Saint-Hilaire. Likewise the Ferrers of Bere Ferrers (yet again an instance of the way in which in the west of England an owner's surname could be tacked on to the place name) derived from Ferrieres in Manche. In passing we can notice the name FitzOsbern, if only to explain that (i) Fitz was by no means the sign of bastardy in every instance and (ii) it was often used in early days without its being a surname at all. FitzOsbern hailed from Breteuil. Foliot is a Norman surname, originally that of a family which began its surname career in the Cotentin and western Normandy.

Gamages comes from Gamaches, Eure. It is a purely Norman surname and gave birth to the familiar Gamage of our time. The loss of the 's' was due no doubt to the slurring over of the pro-nunciation. On the other hand, the loss of the final 's' is fatal, as regards a claim to Norman descent, in the contrasted case of Ferrer, Ferrar and Farrer. All these are ultimately occupational surnames and denote an ancestor who was a farrier or worker in iron, a smith, whereas Ferrers, as mentioned above, is of the gentle Norman blood. (Incidentally why do poets speak of Norman blood as gentle? Not surely in any sense of gentleness of manners. A race who conquered from England to Syria was not likely to be noted for nicety of manners).

Giffard is one of the few instances of a Norman name belonging to one of the companions of the Conqueror, and whose male line descendants are well known in England today. Glanville is purely transported from the south of the Channel, without loss of a single letter. Gournay, in Seine Inférieure, gave the name to the Gurneys. Even more remarkable is the origin of the very English surname of Grenville, or Granville, from Grainville-la-Teinturiere, also in Seine Inférieure. One branch of the family remained in Normandy, the other grew great in England. It is said that the great house of Grenville (one member of which was Sir Richard Grenville of the *Revenge*) is distinct in its beginnings from the family which origi-nated from Grainville, but it is agreed that the Devon Granvilles came from western Normandy. Haig, or de la Haga, came from the district of La Hague in Manche. This seems a very likely origin, although I notice that Scottish genealogists sometimes take the name to derive from haga, an Old English word meaning an en-closure. Be that as it may, the historical family of Haig was Norman.

Harcourt is purely Norman, and there was a castle of Harcourt, the ruins of which existed until 1879. The Hayes are from La Haye-de-Puits. Keynes, and hence Caines, are from Cahagnes, in Calvados. Lacey or Lacy is from Lassy, also in Calvados.

An interesting question is why certain names did not take root in England. For instance, Laval had its representatives in this country in the reign of Henry I. This king gave to one Hugh de Laval property at Pontefract in Yorkshire, but a race of English Lavals has not survived. Lovel, on the other hand, which comes from the Latin *lupus* or wolf, and which derives from Ivry-la-Bataille, did catch on in England and indeed became at one time (late eighteenth and early nineteenth century) a regular name for romance. The Lovels descended from the lords of Ivry. One of the family had a violent temper and was called *lupus* on this account; one of his sons, to distinguish him from his father, was given the diminutive of *lupellus*, hence Lovel. The Lucys, or Luceys, to whom Shakespeare showed some antipathy, because the head of the family, who was a local magistrate, tried him for deer stealing, were of Norman descent, and took their name from Luce, Orne.

One of the oldest Norman families to be connected with England was that of Malet, since their representative was present in this country in the reign of St Edward the Confessor (1042–1066). The name is said to mean 'cursed' or 'accursed'; it is to be distinguished from Martell, which means 'hammer' and which was first bestowed on Charles, father of Pepin the Short, this being Charles, later Martel, who smashed the Saracen army at the battle of Tours in 732. The Malets came from Graville-Sainte-Honorine. They bestowed their name on the Somerset village of Shepton Mallet. Malory, the name borne by the immortal historian of King Arthur and his Knights, is thought to have originated in Tessancourt, in Seine et Oise. The name means 'unfortunate'.

Mandeville, with its variants Manvell, Manville and Manwell, is from Magneville, in Manche, which the tongues of Saxon speakers soon altered to Mandeville. Another family of the same name came from Manneville-sur-Risle. Here is an indication that families bearing the same name often have no connection with each other, simply because in many cases there is more than one place which bestows the surnames. The family of the Queen's Champions, the Dymokes, succeeded to that of Marmion, a name rendered infinitely more famous by Sir Walter Scott's narrative poem. Research has shown that the English Marmions came from Fontenayle-Marmion. Massey or Macey comes from Macey in Manche. Dunham Massey in Cheshire took its second name from them. Mohun, which has turned into Moon and Munn, finds its place of origin in Moyon in Manche, whence they came to the west of England. They were the first owners of Dunster castle, a property which has had only two owners since 1066, the Mohuns and the Luttrells.

Montfort-sur-Risle produced the numerous Montforts, Montfords, Mountforts, Mountfords, Mumfords, Mundfords and Munfords. Saint-Germain-de-Montgomery had curious repercussions in England, for a Welsh county derived its name from the Roger de Montgomery, Earl of Shrewsbury, who accompanied the Conqueror. Whether there is a blood connection between Roger and all those who bear his name is a moot question, to which a negative answer is almost a certainty. Moreville comes from Morville, Mortimer from Mortemer-sur-Eaulne, and Mowbray from Montbrai. It is amusing to reflect on the oft-repeated story that Mortimer comes from some crusading ancestor who had seen the Dead Sea.

There are few names as great in English genealogy as that of Neville, the Earls of Westmorland, whose name comes from Neville in Seine Inférieure. Even when we have discarded the legendary story of Gilbert Neville being the admiral of the Conqueror, we have not only a Norman family, but one which is renowned in every generation of its history. Another mighty family, albeit no longer in the purely male line, is that of Percy, already mentioned in Chapter I, from Percy-en-Auge. Pierrepont comes from a place of that name in Normandy. So, too, does Pomerai, Pomeroy, etc., the family which gave its name to Berry Pomeroy in Devon. This surname was taken from La Pommeraye in Calvados. Port comes from a place called Port-en-Bessin, in Calvados. Poynings is derived from the place of the same name in Sussex, but it is now thought that the family of that name came from Pays de Caux between the forest of Eawy and the Seine. The Punchardons, who gave their name to Heanton Punchardon in Devon, got the original of this English corruption from Pontchardon in Orne.

Many other Norman names may be noted in this survey. Quincy, Raines, Redvers, Romilly, Sackville, St Clair, Saint Hilary, St John, St Leger, St Martin, Saucy, Say (as in the wonderfully sounding Saye and Sele), Scotney, Tankerville, Tilly, Tracy, Tremlett, Vere, Vernon, Villiers, Warenne and Wavell. Some of these names have wound themselves so wonderfully into the very texture of English national life that it is hard to think of them as having come nine centuries ago from across the Channel. Yet so it is, and the explanation of these names is not only interesting to those who bear them, but marvellously illuminating as to the way in which surnames can be twisted into forms very different from their originals. Yet in the cases of St Leger and Vere, the form is not altered, for the former takes its origin from a place named St Leger-aux-Bois, in Seine Inférieure, while Vere is simply Ver in the Manche country. The former name is, of course, that associated with one of the classic English horse races, while Vere has come through a strange series of associations to denote the very quintessence of aristocracy.

The glories of Vere have been chronicled and extolled by no less an historian than Lord Macaulay, they have been sung by Tennyson, and one of the later Vere Earls of Oxford has had the fortune, good or bad, to be chosen as a claimant for the honour of writing Shakespeare; while so high has been the esteem in which Vere of Oxford has been held in peerage circles, than not even a retired Premier was allowed to have the simple Earl of Oxford for his style, but had to be known by the curious hybrid title of Earl of Oxford and Asquith, simply because there might yet be an heir to the dormant or abeyant earldom. The 1086 Aubrey de Vere was an under-tenant of the Bishop of Coutances, in Kensington, Middlesex, and two other places in Northamptonshire. The family of Vere is undoubtedly Norman, but not so renowned in its earlier days as the glory subsequently ascribed to it would lead us to suppose.

The Quincys, who were in earlier times the Earls of Winchester, took their name from Cuinchy in Pas-de-Calais. When they came over with the Conqueror, they were given land in Northamptonshire, only a few miles away from that bestowed upon their immediate overlord, one Anselm de Chokes, whose home in Normandy had been sixteen kilometres from Cuinchy. Raimes or Reames is from Rames in Seine Inférieure. Rennes in Brittany gave rise to the modern Raines and Rains. Reviers, a place in Calvados, was the parent of Redvers. Remilly in Manche produced Rumilly and Romilly. The famous name of Sackville, still in our peerage under Lord Sackville (the Sackville-West family), came from Sauqueville, a little south-west of Dieppe in Normandy. In the

35

Domesday Book the founder of the family in England, Herbrand de Sauqueville, is mentioned as holding Fawley in Buckinghamshire. It is this Herbrand whose visage looks now at the visitors to Knole, the family's great house in Kent. Herbrand is shown in a stained glass window, with a suitable Latin inscription describing him as a companion of the Conqueror.

St Clair, or in the Latin form, de Sancto Claro, hailed from the place of the same name, Saint Clair-sur-Elle, in Manche. In later times a branch of the family settled in Scotland and the name then took the form (though not the pronunciation) of Sinclair. It became a Caithness surname, though the first Scottish possession was in Roslin, near Edinburgh, famous for being mentioned in Sir Walter Scott's poems.

Saint Hilary, or St Hilaire, de Sancto Hilario, comes from Saint Hilaire-du-Harcouët. The well-known surname St John (pronounced Sinjohn, though no one has ever read a lesson from the Gospel according to Sinjohn), is from St Jean-le-Thomas and thus is only a translation into English. St Martin, de Sancto Martino, is from Saint Martin-le-Gaillard, and the Martin family of Devon have given their name, in the west country fashion mentioned above, to Combe Martin. Saucy is from La Saussaye, Eure. They, too, bestowed their surname upon the place in which they lived in England, taking it from Normandy and adding it to the English name of the locality—Newbold Saucy in Leicestershire. Here again we note, that on arrival in England, the Saucy who had been vassal to one Ives de Harcourt in Normandy held the same relationship for his lands in England.

Saye and Sele is one of the most picturesque titles in the whole of the peerage. One is not surprised to learn that its holder now is the twentieth Baron. The family is without question Norman and the name of the title (the family name has become Twisleton-Wykeham-Fiennes) is derived from Sai, Orne, arr. and cant. of Argentan.

Scotney is the English form of Etocquigny in Seine Inférieure. How easily a surname could be changed is shown by the case of Robert de Tosny, in Eure, whose surname in England became Robert de Stafford after the name of his English holding. The great house of Tankerville is from Tancarville in Seine Inférieure. Tilly comes from Tilly-sur-Seulles. Tracy, already mentioned, has not been easy to place, but some authorities think that there is much to be said for Tracy-sur-Mer (Calvados). Vernon of Haddon in Eure has the honour of producing the well-known Vernons of Haddon Hall, famous in romance and history alike. The equally famous Villiers family takes its surname from Villiers-le-Sec in Calvados. Warenne is from Varenne, and the great family of the Earl Warenne arose from this place. Wavell, the name of the great soldier who gained the first land victories for Britain in the Second World War, comes from Vauville in the Cotentin peninsula.

The mention of the name Warenne as being genuinely Norman gives occasion for a caution, since the name can also have come from a person who kept a warren. This would be a servant or lower official, who was responsible for the warren of rabbits. It is often said that rabbits were introduced into this country by the Normans and were originally kept in warrens, under the charge of an official. So if your name is Warren, you may not be the descendant of the ancient earl, but of an official or keeper of rabbits for some great lord.

Before anyone, who bears any of the names quoted above as Norman, prides himself upon being Norman, he should consider his genealogy. To my knowledge there are about two hundred of the county families of England who can honestly claim to be Norman. For reasons which are not difficult to grasp, few persons can claim a male line of descent from someone who was at Hastings. The names of only a few warriors at that battle are known to us, after an exhaustive search by scholars, and they are fewer than thirty in number, all told, including those who are mentioned as being killed and who left no offspring. In any event those with whom the country was settled and colonised twenty years after Hastings, and whose names occur as tenants in Domesday Book (1086), would not by any means be synonymous with those of the fighters at Hastings (1066). One has only to reflect that the men who were in the first wave at the Normandy beaches in 1944 did not normally hold the executive posts in the commissions which governed the liberated countries some years later. So, too, with the Norman invaders; the bravest knights would not of necessity be thought suitable to rule England in positions which required considerable skill and tact, as well as experience and administrative ability.

Domesday Book is not in any case a genealogical record. It sets out the land holding of England; by what persons the country was settled and held; what wealth they possessed; and what fighting

37

force they could put into the field at the king's bidding. Genealogy comes in only by accident. It is not until some sixty years later that it becomes possible to assign a father and son relationship in the great families of feudal England, with the first appearance of the Great Roll of the Pipe. This is the record of the royal revenue, and the name is derived from the fact that the record is written on a roll wound round a stick or pipe. For nearly seven hundred years these rolls continued, and as they formed records of taxation on the landed property they were often occupied with records which showed the succession to estates.

One series begins in the reign of Henry I (1100–1135), more than a generation after Hastings or even Domesday. Consequently, it is not in the overwhelming majority of cases possible to prove Norman ancestry back to the actual Conquest. It is essential to get the facts about Norman descent right in this book, because the beginning of surnames is from the Normans. Unless it is understood how hard it is to connect a family back to 1086, many people will be tempted to think of themselves as Norman, whereas they merely bear a Norman name. (See also Chapter 10.)

Suppose someone is called Tilly or Vernon. Does this mean that he or she is descended from a Norman lord, who came to the settlement of England in time to have fat lands and houses recorded in Domesday? If what I have said about the change of names is borne in mind, it will be clear that many surnames now used have been assumed in the past, however far back that may be. The fluidity in the use of surnames makes this certain. How did names come to be changed? Very often through personal preference. The same thing constantly occurred over coats of arms. In the days of Queen Victoria, a certain British ambassador to the United States had his coach in Washington bearing his elaborate coat of arms. This went into a coach-makers for repair, and while there was noted by an admiring American gentleman. He thought that the decoration on the coach was mighty fine and ordered the same for himself. The result was that the thing caught on and soon half-a-dozen versions of the Ambassador's coat of arms were to be seen on the city streets. Similarly, many a man or woman born Ramsbotham has admired a more high-sounding name, with the sequel that this surname has been quietly assumed and the other dropped.

Then again, I believe, though I cannot prove, that in many cases surnames were assumed in old days from motives of admiration and

38

flattery by servants, who may have begun by being styled 'Mr Cary's man,' and then gradually dropped the addition and been known simply as Cary.

The idea of Norman descent is a vast delusion in the majority of instances. Those who contend most about it are the least likely to have it. The very extravagance of their claims to Norman blood shows that they cannot substantiate it. One person says that he or she descends from the man who bore the Conqueror's standard at Hastings. Judging by the number of claimants for this honour, which was in fact very hard to bestow on the morning of the actual battle, there must have been relief riders coming up every five minutes to take the flag. The Conqueror's shield has been another favourite grip for ancestor-seeking would-be Normans. The Fitz-William family claim a scarf given to the Hastings ancestor by William. Incidentally, the surname of this noble house is no claim upon the Bastard of Normandy's body. FitzWilliam means simply the son of William, and the ancestry of this truly great house shows that at its foot there is a right English man, one Godric, whose son was named William, and grandson FitzWilliam. It had become the fashion to give Norman or French baptismal names, and Fitz was the Norman equivalent of the Welsh 'Ap', the Irish 'O' and the Highland 'Mac', meaning 'son of'.

Perhaps one of the most amusing derivations of a surname is that of Airdale or Iredale. A man who fought on William's side at Hastings bore simply a Christian name—e.g. Piers. In the course of the battle, he was borne down, but William commanded the crowd to give him air. Afterwards he adopted the surname of Air (Ayre) in compliment to his regal benefactor. Then he was given some land in a dale, hence Airedale.

Some would-be Normans refer to the Battle Abbey Roll. What is the truth about this? That there was some sort of Roll I do not doubt. After all, William had promised that if he were victorious in the fight, he would build an abbey on the spot of the victory. This vow he fulfilled and Battle Abbey arose on the site of the battle. I would not be surprised if the monks had kept a Roll of those for whose souls they were to pray. In fact, they not only kept such a Roll, but had blank spaces in it, for the names of later benefactors to be inserted. The consequence of this forethought on the part of the monks was that the Roll must have come to include many names of benefactors to the abbey whose connection with the actual battle, in their own person or in that of their ancestors, was precisely nil. When the monasteries were dissolved, there were six lists or purported copies of the original list, which were set out by antiquarians, such as Leland. How much authenticity can be granted to any of these lists is now impossible to determine, but two facts can be taken as definite: (i) there was an original Roll from which the six versions were taken; (ii) many names on the Roll as it now appears have no Norman or even French origin. (See also Chapter 10.)

I have dwelt at some length on this subject of Norman ancestry because the Normans were the first to use surnames in this country, and hence many people assume that they are of Norman origin because their names are of continental provenance. The names which I have gone through above do not by any means exhaust the quota of Norman names, but it must be remembered that it was not only the Norman lords who came over. They brought with them their dependants and followers. Many names of Norman or French origin are mingled in our language without their being of necessity those of great persons.

Argent is said by some authorities to be a shortened form of Argentan; by others it is considered to be a nickname, derived from the possession of silvery locks. Charters and Charteris come from Chartres; Bullen or Bollen or Boleyn are from Boulogne; possibly Gant or Gent are from Ghent; and in a few cases Legge is not from its natural meaning of 'leg' (some form of nickname), but from Liége. Rumney is thought to be connected with Romanee in Burgundy, a celebrated wine district.

In these cases, though, we may be sure that there was no place of a great or even a mesne lordship, from which proud Norman knights came to the conquest and spoliation of England.

I have written also on these Norman names, because of the enormous interest and pride in Normanity which the top people of this country, and all who aspire to the top, display in the subject. In my book, *They Came with the Conqueror*, I went through both the *Peerage* and the *Landed Gentry*, analysing the names of the families and showing those which could reasonably claim Norman descent, and, by inference at least, those which could not. It was rather amusing to note that those who were accorded the accolade of Normanity were inclined to think the book very, very good, while others whose Norman claim had been knocked out could hardly bring themselves to speak about the subject. It is this strange interest in and respect for a set of brutal conquerors which always fascinates me in studying the Norman Conquest, because clearly it is not a dead and gone piece of history, but something which is living now in the minds of many English folk. In order to get to the bottom of this subject I have written another work, already published, on the history of the Conquest and its meaning in the various departments of our national life to the present day.

In this chapter I have followed, with certain exceptions, the instances given by L. C. Loyd, whose book, *The Origins of Some Anglo-Norman Families*, I have already mentioned. This fine work has been as finely edited by two distinguished scholars, Charles Travis Clay, formerly librarian of the House of Lords, and David C. Douglas, the editor of Eyre and Spottiswoode's great series of *English Historical Documents*. Much other valuable information can be gleaned from *Burke's Peerage* and *Burke's Landed Gentry*. Bardsley is as usual very useful; many of his explanations differ from those of the more modern works, but are none-the-less well worth studying. It may well be that, in certain cases, there are two possible derivations of a surname, which as we shall see later follow two different lines of descent.

III. Place Names

In ford, in ham, in ley, in ton,
The most of English surnames run.

In support of which jingle we may cite the fact that of the surnames
of fifteen Premiers in this century, nearly half are of local origin—
namely, Home (a name of a place in Scotland, but of English origin
since the Scottish lowlands are largely English in their original
colonisation), Eden, Churchill, Attlee, Bonar Law (the latter being
the name of a hill or burial mound in Old English), Asquith (the
form which Askwith took in certain cases), Balfour, to which could
be added Primrose, a place name in Scotland from which the family
of the Earls of Rosebery derives its name.

What is true of the names of Premiers is true of almost any other
list. In the previous chapter, I pointed out that many of the names
which were first borne in this country as surnames, and which
came ready-made from abroad, were names of places in Normandy
or some other part of France. When surnames began to be adopted
generally in England it was very natural for the place of a man's
birth or principal residence to be given to him as the distinguishing
mark. Many names which were at first simply 'of' such and such a
place have been joined to the first name and thus are now looked
upon as a surname. Few people refer to Thomas of Aquinum, but
to St Thomas Aquinas, yet the distinguishing name of the saint, to
mark him out from the other Thomases of his age, and later of the
Church's calendar, was taken from the place of his birth. Matthew
Paris was simply Matthew of Paris; similarly, John of Salisbury,
William of Ockham and so on. In the same way surnames taken
from these sources became extremely common.

What are the sources of English local names? No one has written
more learnedly on this subject than the Swede, Eilert Ekwall (d.

1964), whose work, *The Concise Oxford Dictionary of English Place Names*, is in its third edition. He said: 'The English place nomenclature is composite, place names being derived from various sources. This sometimes renders a definite etymology difficult. The majority of place names are English, but there are not a few Celtic names, a great many Scandinavian, and some Latin and French names. A number of hybrid names occur' (p. xix). Here we are concerned with the majority of names being English. Why is this? Particularly as the names of the greater rivers and streams are to a large extent British, and many small streams also have British names. Yet there are a considerable number of river and stream names of English origin, while most small streams have English names.

It is one of the great—possibly the greatest—unsolved mysteries of English history, which is here presented to us in thinking of the origin of our place names. For four centuries the Romans were in control of this country, as of Wales and the lowlands of Scotland. This country was the Roman province of Britain. Yet how few Roman names (mostly those ending in -caster or -cester) are found in our local nomenclature. They appear like curiosities. The overwhelming number of English local names are of English origin.

Did, then, the invading English in the fifth and sixth centuries just take over the land, and in the theory formerly dominant in English history books, wipe out or chase away into the west the Romano-British inhabitants, and then carry out a colonisation of the whole land, so that Britain became England? This is what we should be led to expect, save for that awkward fact about the river names, and more so still the names of small streams in some cases. Avon is an example in full view. Does one learn the name of the local river before drowning one's enemies in it? Does one ask of a victim, before cutting his throat, what is the name of the river by which he has lived?

It seems odd. Yet it could have happened, perhaps in this way. In most of the provinces of the Roman Empire, which were overrun by the Germanic tribes, these same invaders had already learned much about the lands which they came to conquer. They had usually had relatives in the imperial armies; often they had served in the Roman forces themselves. Or they had travelled in the Roman lands as traders, who could turn their hands usefully to piracy or robbery when the time offered the opportunity. As Charles Kingsley once remarked, the Roman Empire was like a vast trolls' garden, into

43

which the noble barbarians from Germany occasionally penetrated, and from which they did not always get back with unsullied
souls. That at least was the way in which he looked at the matter;
not quite the viewpoint of Hilaire Belloc in *Europe and the Faith*.
Anyway, a certain knowledge of older names for great natural
objects could have seeped into the language of the Germanic invaders of Britain.

Leaving this on one side, however, I think the fact that place
after place, small places that is, had English names, and especially
that the smaller streams often had names of English origin,
does point to the massacre or driving away of the bulk of the original inhabitants. The population of Roman Britain must have
been fairly large, even if we assume (which cannot be proved) that
Caesar's estimate of the British population had been grossly ex-
aggerated four hundred years before the Roman province came to
an end. It would seem strange if the population of a settled province of an empire powerful and flourishing should have declined.

Yet if only the names of largish natural features such as the
greater waterways outlasted the English conquest, the natural inference is that the former inhabitants did not survive the English
settlement, though they may not all have been killed. We can take
the analogy of the Northmen and their settlement over much of
north-eastern England in the times of the Viking invasions. A large
element of Scandinavian naming came into English. One familiar
example is the use of the ending—by, as in Grimsby, or Whitby,
meaning a cliff. Whitby, indeed, is only one instance of a place
which had its English name changed for the Viking appellation.

There is a wonderful romance in the fact that a name such as
Bodiam, meaning the ham or home or little township of one Bod,
has lasted for nearly fifteen centuries. Who was this Bod? One is
almost tempted to fall back upon modern slang for the answer. Or
what of the person whose name gave its title to the smallest
English county, Rota? Of him the latest reference work says: 'Who
Rota was and when he lived we may never know.' It is over nine
hundred years since Rutlandshire was regarded as the dowry of
English queens. By the time of Edward the Confessor (1042–1066)
it was settled custom that the lands of Rota should be the Queen's
dowry. Who was the original Rota?

The period from 411 (when the Romans officially withdrew,
somewhat in the manner in which we can be said to have with-

drawn from India), until 597, when St Augustine came on his mission to make Angels out of Angles, is the darkest in our long history. We have very little written evidence—hardly anything besides
some sermon tracts of St Gildas—and the archaeological evidence
is not conclusive one way or the other, either for or against the
destruction of the Romano-Britons. So we are at liberty to use our
imagination, in trying to pierce the gloom which surrounds our
Saxon or, as I prefer to say, our English ancestors. We can then
think of some chieftain from the heaths of Denmark, or the swampy
waters of the Elbe, saying goodbye for ever to his boyhood home and
setting out for the land of Britain. Then leaving his boats on the
shore or burning them when he had gone as far as he could navi-
gate up the rivers, he struck inland. He would leave the nearby
Roman town or villa—we know that the Saxons seldom dwelt in the
actual buildings of the vanished race—and set up his homestead in
this new land.

In its way this migration of the ancestors of the English race
bears resemblance to the colonisation of the hitherto trackless
wilderness of North America by the descendants of these same
early English. There must have been disasters, as there were in
America, when bands of settlers may have fallen victim to Romano-
British vengeance (the legends of Arthur and his Round Table are
the folk lore reminiscence of a great British *revanche* against the
Saxons), been killed in inter-tribal conflicts, or even been over-
whelmed by wolves, or other savage creatures which began to
swarm as the land was deserted by its inhabitants.

None-the-less these small bands did settle down and then vanish
from history, save for the name which they left behind. Thus
Beddington, in Surrey, the ton or town of the Beddings. Wellington
in Somerset, given as Walintone in Domesday Book, must have
been the home of some group of the Wellings or of one person
Welling, a small leader of settlers. How strange that Wellington
should have become one of the proudest titles in the whole of the
British aristocracy.

Some of the larger groupings of settlers have left their mark on
our land, and hence on our surnames. Thus Essex of the East
Saxons, Wessex of the West Saxons, Sussex of the South Saxons,
Middlesex of the Middle Saxons, and so on. In the north, we have
Northumberland; East Anglia on the east; with Mercia on the
west and in the midland shires. Kent, another kingdom of the

45

ever-shifting Heptarchy, is a name older than the English conquest
and goes back to Cantium. Kentish is, however, part French or
Norman and partly English in derivation, since both languages
have similar forms. Many of the shires have contributed to our
nomenclature. Wiltshire reflects the occasion when a person left
the country to settle elsewhere. A man was not so likely to be called
'of' some particular area until he left it, when he would be distinguished from his new neighbours as a foreigner from another
part of the country, even though that part was only a few score
miles away.

It is curious that the name of the second largest English city
should have sprung from a settlement of some obscure Berming,
whose ham was for ages little more than a hamlet. Liverpool and
Manchester also, for centuries from their foundation, were only
tiny places. As Dr Bardsley remarks: 'Mushroom-like they sprung
up but yesterday, while for centuries these insignificant hamlets
have pursued the even tenor of their way, somewhat disturbed, it
may have been, from their equanimity four or five centuries ago,
by the announcement that Ralph or Miles was about to leave them,
and who, by thus becoming "Ralph de Debenham" or "Miles de
Ashford" have given to the world to the end of time the story of
their early departure'.

It is not only the rude forefathers of the hamlet who for ever
sleep in obscurity. Some hamlets have been destined never to
achieve any fame. Even more cruel is the fate of a place such as
Piltdown, in Sussex, which passed over a millennium in decent
obscurity, to win fame only some fifty years back, and to have its
name inscribed in the world's register of science, then to be discovered to be the place of a well-planned fraud. The Piltdown Man
must rank in scientific literature with the Forged Decretals, only
unfortunately the credulous in this twentieth century were not
ignorant and barbarous fighters and barons, but the flower of the
world's scientists—all deceived by a conglomeration of disparate
bones! Truly science hath her defeats no less than those of religion. Alas for the Piltdown savage painted on the local inn sign!
Alas for fame so long in coming, only to be forgotten save for a
gibe for the rest of time!

In tracing your surnames, then, you can take it that there is no
place, however obscure, in this country which has not given its
name to some person or persons, some family or tribe. The mean-

ing of these names does not vary greatly. Those ending in -cester are derived from the Latin *castra* and must denote either a fortified Roman site, such as Chester, or else one which was later strengthened by the English in defence against the Danes. The numerous burghs are from the old English name for a fortified place, while the boroughs have much the same meaning. Ford, ham and ton have already been explained or need little explanation. Ley or leigh means a clearing in a wood.

Anyone who possesses a name which can be identified with a place in one of our gazetteers can be sure that he is half way to an explanation of the meaning of his surname. For the English place names have received a great deal of attention, and not unnaturally they were among the first to be given a true derivation, while many of them have retained this meaning from early times. It is doubtful if anyone ever failed to know the meaning of Chester, or Gloucester, or Worcester. Possibly they did not mistake the origin of Birmingham, but this is more doubtful, because Birmingham, like many other places in the middle ages, became the seat of a great family. The Berminghams (the difference of the vowel in spelling is unimportant, since change in the spelling of English words has been common for ages), were a great family who somehow managed to leave their grandeur in the sixteenth and seventeenth centuries, though there are many families who think themselves descended from them, and who quite possibly are, if they could only find the relevant documents. Consequently, it may well have been thought that the De Berminghams had given their name to the place where they lived, instead of having adopted the name of some Saxon chieftain or tribe lost in the mists of unchronicled time.

Having found that one's name is that of a place, often of a very small, obscure place, one is thrown back upon the meaning of the place name. Some of these, which are very common, have been explained already, but there are many other prefixes and suffixes in place names which require an explanation. Many of them are properly Celtic or at least non-English in their meaning. Scottish, Irish and Welsh names will be dealt with later in full; meanwhile, it would be convenient to note such forms as aber, which means the mouth of a river, as in Aberford, Berwick, or Barmouth. In Gaelic the word all means white, hence the significance of Aln (as in Alnwick), Alan, Ellen or Lune. Avon, meaning a river, can be found in other forms, as Evan, Ive, Anne (this could be the origin

47

of the place name Ann in Hampshire), and Inney. Ayr is Norse for beach. Bach in Welsh means little. Balder is the name of the old Norse god who has been made familiar by Matthew Arnold's poem and which is enshrined in the name of Balderton. The common ben of the Highlands of Scotland is Gaelic for a hilltop. Bel can mean a ford or entrance of a river, hence Belfast. Blair means a field, hence the numerous Blairs of Scotland, who have so often penetrated to the south of England. The very frequent borough means a fortified place and gained great currency during the period of the English recovery in the tenth century against the Danes. A burn is a stream; a brae is a top or summit; bryn is a brow or ridge, as in Brandon, Birnwood. By or byr is Scandinavian for a dwelling place, and can give such names as Aylesbere, Beer Alston, etc.

Sometimes the derivation of many of our oldest place names cannot be worked out exactly, though it can be agreed that they are pre-English conquest. Thus London as a name preceded even the Roman conquest. The Roman form was, of course, Londinium, but the original name was Celtic and meant either a fort or the place by the pool.

The struggles and survival of various races to form Great Britain, or the United Kingdom, is reflected in the language and the names of places all over the British Isles. Caer is the Welsh form of the Roman *castra*, and is appropriate in Caernarvon, Carlisle or Carstairs. In most of these places, the name was derived from the natural strength of the situation, and the modern fortification or medieval castle was merely the latest fortification of the site. Cairn is a heap of stones, as indeed the word has preserved its meaning in modern English; Carnlea, or Carron, is an example. Cann means head or top and has a wide distribution, in names like Kinsale, Kenmare, Kintyre or Kencot.

Cefn, the Welsh for ridge, has given us such typically English names as Cheviot, Keynton and Chevy Chase, which last Sir Philip Sidney declared he could never hear without his heart being stirred. Chipping is Old English for a place where things were bought—i.e. a market—as in Chepstow or Chipping. This came from the Old English verb to buy, ceapian, which was also the source of our Chapmans. Clere in old English meant a residence for some important person; Clough was Irish for a stone, as in Claughton; Coch, so often found in Welsh names, means red and occurs in a feminine form as goch. Lincoln is said to be derived

from the Latin *colonia,* or colony. Combe is found in both English
and Welsh, meaning a bowl-shaped valley; Compton and Gom-
shall find here their ancestor.

Den or dene is a deep wooded valley or swine pasture, and this
is thought to be the origin of the place name Croydon. Croft is an
enclosed field, and it is easy to think of many derivatives in our
surnames. Field itself is originally a forest clearing, where the trees
have been felled. Daire or Doire is an oak wood, as in London-
derry; dale is Norse for a valley, and can sometimes be found
altered to dal, as in Kendal, Arundel or Oundle. Don is supposed
to be connected with the Celtic avon; donn, however, is brown or
dun. Esk is Gaelic for water and is found in a variety of forms, as
in Esk, Usk, Exe, Ouse and possibly in the -es of Thames. Ey
means an island and many forms of this are found, as in the well
known Bermondsey, 'Bermonds' island'. Who could this Bermond
have been? The question becomes the more fascinating from the
impossibility of ever finding an answer.

Fell, a mountain, is from Scandinavian. Fiord, again, which
occurs in such well known names as Wexford or Carlingford, is
another Norse name, the same as the Scottish firth, or opening.
Ford is in origin simply the same name, but from Old English, as
in Bideford, where the word has its true meaning. Garth, as in
Garthwaite, means an enclosed place, or yard, and is Norse. The
English ham means an enclosure or home. Holm, so frequent an
ending to many surnames, is Scandinavian and English for a river
island, such as in Steepholm, the island off the Somerset coast.
Holt is English for a copse, hurst for a thick wood. Ley is English
for a clearing in the forest and is found in the form Leigh. As the
early English settlers had to hew their way through thick forests
and use the cleared land for their crops, it can be imagined how
easy it was for this suffix to occur in our language.

Loch is, of course, Gaelic for lake or arm of the sea. Mark is
Old English for a boundary or frontier, as in Merkbury or March-
mont. Mere is English for lake, and it is curious how this word has
lived on, in English poetic language, so that its use there is now
almost sacrosanct. Windermere or Grasmere is an instance of its
use in names. Some writers give or from ora, a shore, as the source
of Windsor, which I mentioned earlier as being in dispute between
scholars. Over in English also meant a shore, as in Wendover.

Prest was Old English for priest, as in Prestbury, the latter part meaning a burying place as with Bury St Edmunds. Rugeley, or Reigate, owe their names to old English rudge, a ridge or back. Set is Old English from seta, meaning a settlement. The famous soke of Peterborough, or of Thorp le Soken, is Old English for a local court. Staple is a market. Sten is old Norse for a stone, and examples occur in Stenton or Stennis. Tod, a fox, appears in Todburn and Todfield. Tor, as in Torquay or Dunster, is a tower or pinnacle of rock. Wark, as in Southwark, is a fortress and is old Norse. Ware means the inhabitants of, as in Worcester, which thus combines with the old Roman *castra*. Weald is Old English for a woodland and can be found in the form Waltham. Wick is a village or a marsh, as in Wickham. Yard is a place guarded or girded about. By contrast to these English words, we have ville or well, the French for an abode. French place names have come into the language as anyone can see by recalling names such as Beauchamp.

William Camden, who began the study of our surnames some four hundred years ago, gives a list of names derived from places in England. This he does after referring to surnames derived from places on the Continent, and goes on to add (*Remaines*, etc., p. 119 edition of 1870): 'From places in England and Scotland infinite likewise. For every town, village, or hamlet hath afforded names to families: as Derbyshire, Lancashire, Essex, Murray, Clifford, Stafford, Barkley [by way of comment I may add that Barclay and Berkeley are the same name, though spelt differently, the English original being Berkeley, the Scottish branch Barclay], Leigh, Lea, Hastings [of course from Hastings in most cases, but also possibly a patronymic, from Hastang, a Norman personal name], Hamleton, Gordon, Lumley, Douglas, Booth, Clinton, Heydon, Cleydon, Hicham [this must be the modern Hitcham], Henningham, Popham, Ratcliffe, Markham, Seaton, Framingham, Pagrave, Cotton, Carie, Hume, Poinings, Goring, Prideaux [a place in Cornwall], Windsor, Hardes, Stanhope, Sydenham, Needham, Dimoc [Dymoke], Winnington, Allington, Dacre, Thaxton, Whitney, Willoughby, Apseley, Crew, Kniveten, Wentworth, Fanshaw, Woderington, Manwood, Fetherston, and lastly Penruddock, Tremain, Trevoire, Killigrew, Roscarrec, Carminow, and most families in Cornwall, of whom I have heard this rhyme:

> *By Tre, Ros, Pol, Lan, Caer, and Pen,*
> *You may know the most Cornish men.*

Which signifies a town, a heath, a pool, a church, a castle, or city, and a foreland, or promontory.' I shall return to Cornish names in Chapter 10.

The name of Carminow was still borne in Camden's time by a distinguished west country family; this family had had a quarrel with the Scropes of Richard II's reign and had come out of the dispute with their ancestral coat of arms which had been the same as Scrope's. In the seventeenth century it seems that the Carminow family died out in the male, though still represented in the *Landed Gentry* in the female line. I should hesitate, however, to say that any name is extinct in this country, because so often there are obscure relatives of some notable family, and if one says that a line is extinct there tend to come forth scions of the old house to prove that they still bear the name with honour if not with riches.

From this list given by Camden it may be seen that a multitude of names is taken from places into our nomenclature of surnames. As he goes on to observe, many of these places are quite unknown to all but the most determined of gazetteer makers—often unknown even to the bearers of the names themselves.

Since the purpose of this book is to give outlines or hints by which a man or woman may work out his or her own surname's meaning, rather than to attempt a dictionary, I shall not try to go on through list after list of the surnames, current in England, which come from places.

Suffice it to add that names like Green are often derived from a place, although it can also come from the sense of being immature or young, in which instance it would be from a nickname. This explanation of Green does get over the difficulty which attaches to 'colour' surnames. Why White, Black, Brown, Red, but no Purple or Yellow? If Green is derived from 'at the Green' then there need be no difficulty in wondering why only certain colours were used as nicknames or why Green should have been selected to furnish a nickname and not Yellow or Purple.

I would remind readers that there are two classes of place names —those derived from an actual place which can be identified today, or which did once exist, with a local habitation and a name, and the second class which is taken from some physical characteristic, such a meadow, or a clearing in the woods, or a hill, or some other feature which called for a description, but which never became distinguished by the presence of even a hamlet to give it immortality.

From the above it will be seen that there is a huge class of surnames which come from places, and the inquirer should make certain in the first place that he has got the name correctly derived from such and such a place. If the place has lived as well as his name, then it is probable that the spelling may now be the same, though this does not always follow as we have seen in the instances of Debenham (now Deadman) or Godliman from Godalming. Amersham, as I have said, is the modern form of Agmondisham and there may be some family somewhere still bearing the name in the old spelling. The old spelling of Bristol—Bristow (the bridge head)—has contributed a number of Bristows (Bristowes), also possibly Bristos, to our surnames.

Of course, there are plenty of instances of a surname being in existence now which is derived from a place long defunct, like Goldsmith's *Deserted Village*. These instances must provide some of the most difficult etymological problems, unless by diligent search we can find some record of the now vanished village or hamlet. This may be the case eventually with Imber, in Wiltshire, which the War Office has made into a deserted village and the name of which may ultimately be replaced on the map by a grid reference or army number.

There is a further class of surnames which are undoubtedly taken from places, but which cannot be traced here, in our own gazetteers. These are the names of foreign places. We began this part of our study by tracing the Norman and French names which came over following the Norman invasion in 1066. Subsequent centuries brought many more. The principal immigrations are those of French persons, not connected with the Conquest, but with the influx of favourites of various kings, such as Henry III. He was particularly favourable to Poitevins, hence, by the way, the curious name, Portwine, which has nothing to do with drink, but represents a long forgotten ancestor against whom our English forbears fulminated, but who managed to settle here and become an Englishman.

After the loss of Normandy, fewer foreigners could have come in than during the long connection with that part of France. It has to be remembered, however, that after King John lost Normandy in 1204, the English possessions in western France went on for some two hundred and fifty years, until in 1453 the French at last succeeded in expelling the English from Gascony and Bordeaux.

This very long connection with England led to many persons having, as it were, a dual nationality and bringing their blood and names into England. Champagne is a case in point, and the variants of Portugal which are given nowadays as Pettengell, Petteingill, Pettingale, Pettingall and Puttergill. The form Portingale also survives. Reverting to Portwin or Portwine, this, derived from Poitevin, has been found also as Puddifant or Puttifant.

Spain is another surname derived from an ancestor, who either came from that country or had business with it. Dr Reaney gives another interpretation, however, deriving the name from Espnay for some one who may have come from that place. Pickar is from Picardy, and Champagne from that district of France. An interesting case, which we shall meet later, is that of Wallace, which is thought to derive from le Wallis, a Welshman, and hence a foreigner originally in the Scotland of the middle ages. A strange name for the great patriot of Scotland.

Sarson is a form of Saracen, and may denote someone descended from a Saracen captive, as in the familiar story of the ancestry of St Thomas of Canterbury. On the other hand, it may mean only that an ancestor had a dark complexion. Mention of Thomas à Becket introduces another form of the place name, and a more common one than that derived from a place which exists or did once exist. Becket could be from the little known place Beckett in Berkshire, but more likely from the little stream or beck. At the beck became 'Frenchified' into à Becket. There are many examples of this in our medieval literature. At wood became Atwood, at Lee Attlee. Attenborough is from atte borough, Atterbury being another form of this name. As soon as one begins to think of this type of name, many others occur—Atworth, Atcliffe, etc. According to Dr Bardsley, Agate comes from att-gate and Amor from Atte-more. Noakes is from Atte-oakes and Nash from Atten-ash. Similarly the prefix -by has been used to form surnames, so that Bywaters, and Bywoods, show that the ancestor lived by the waters or by the wood.

It will occur to most people that the common forms Townshend or Townend are from a place source, the end of the town. Lanes, Fields, Woods, Holmes, Street, Streeter, Brookes, all attest their origin from some little feature of the landscape which marked the residence of the ancestor. The fairly common form Mountain is also derived from a long past ancestor's residence near a mountain. Mount again denotes someone living by a small elevation.

53

Hurst has given rise to a large family of unrelated surnames. Shaw, too, has been a great enricher of our nomenclature. The numerous forms of Shaw which we meet—Cockshaw, Ramshaw, Hindshaw and so on—are fairly clear in their meaning, but what is the parentage of Shawcross? Is it a corruption from some form of ordinary Shaw? Or does it represent Shacklecross near Derby?

Den and ley have given rise to numerous surnames, so that many Cowleys, Cowdens, Buckdens and Hartleys or Oxleys can find in this ending of the name the explanation of their surnames. The well-known name Slade means a valley and hence belongs to the great class of place names. There are many variants of slade, which is an Old English word, as anyone can recollect who has heard of Greenslades, or Sladen, which means a hollow in the wood. Launde gives many other surnames; according to Bardsley it means 'a pretty and rich piece of grassy sward in the heart of a forest'. Hence, Lowndes, or Laundes.

In other cases the place name has been slightly disguised by having an 's' added, so that it appears as Holmes, or Holmans, or Knowles, Hills, Cliffes. Fairclough, for instance, means fair cliff. Combe or Downe need little explanation, the meaning springing at once to mind. Each of such endings bring with it also numerous other names, such as Thorncombe, Lipcombe, Woolcombe, etc. Heath, from an obvious source, is also represented by Heth. It is, by the way, a humdrum ending to what at first sight appears to be a somewhat romantic name, for could not the Heths be the children of Heth, the old Biblical form? It is similarly disconcerting to note that Pharaoh, as we shall see under occupational surnames, comes from Farrar and has nothing to do with ancient Egypt. A name which does retain an element of romance is that of Gorges, which is a genuine Norman name, innocent of all connection with the Conquest, because the family of this name came over from Normandy only as late as the reign of King John, after the loss to the English Crown of Normandy in 1204. Gorges is represented in the family coat of arms by a whirlpool, a very effective bearing, derived from the fact that *gurges* in Latin means a whirlpool, or fountain, this being a play upon the name. Possibly this family did take its name from a place where there was a troubled spring.

Gore, the name of a noble family in the British aristocracy, has a curious etymology, for the word *gara* in Old English means a triangular piece of land, and thus at some unrecorded period the

54

founder of this noble line must have lived in a small way by some three-sided plot, which formed his simple support.

Numerous names come from trees, such as Quince, Oakley, Vine, Ash, or Ashley, Thorne, Broome, but not Pine, which is admittedly a place name but has little to do with the tree which forms the heraldic pun on the name in most of the Pine (or Pyne) coats of arms.

Croft means a meadow, which combines with Bancroft (or Beancroft), Haycroft, Meadowcroft. Yard is found in Appleyard. A hay is an edge and has formed a powerful surname for a Scottish clan, beside giving many name forms in southern Britian. Hayley is one of the most common, Haywood or Heywood another.

These place names often give us a sense of the difficulties which arise in tracing the origin of our surnames. Take as an instance that of Trappes-Lomax, the name of a modern family whose pedigree is traced back, in the Trappes line at least, for a full five hundred years. Trappes, I am told by one of the modern representatives, who should certainly be in a position to know, since he is Somerset Herald of the College of Arms, means a short, thickset fellow. Right into the fourteenth century this surname can be traced, and then is lost, though it is to be hoped that further research may yet uncover the original short, thickset fellow. The other half of the name, Lomax, is a place name and is traced through various forms— Lomas, Lummus, Loomis, as well as Loomas and Lomax—back to a place which is now lost. This was Lomax, which earlier appeared as Lumhalghs, and was the name of an area south of Bury in Lancashire. How many more such examples could be found! It must indeed prove puzzling to the researcher who does not know that the place which gave his ancestors their name has vanished from the map. These names are traced very often from appearing in old records as parts of the names—thus, John de Lummis.

On the other hand, what surprises there are in store for some name bearers—e.g. the Conyers, or Conners, whose name is deduced by etymologists from *le convers* or convert, this meaning a converted Jew in the middle ages. I often wonder how some of the foreign surnames, now so plentiful in England, will fare if they are gradually abbreviated or slurred over by the careless English, so that Jasienski becomes Jestneck. I should not be surprised, for many similar changes have taken place in our nomenclature.

The numerous class of Thorpes owe their name to thorpe, a

village, hence the multitude of Thorpes, Winthorpes (also Winthrop), Calthorp, or Westropps, whom we meet. The well-known ending bury, meaning a place of a borough, was often Normanised into *de la bere*, so that thence we get not only some modern de la Beres (the ending of the name of a recent Lord Mayor of London), but also Berrys, Berrimans and Beares. Sale is a name going back into the middle ages, when the Sale family were landowners. They derive their name from an old English word, meaning sallow, a name used for a species of salix or willow. Many names are metamorphosed out of all likely connection with their first bearer's place of residence, or as it subsequently turned out, his occupation. Thus Conybeare is a name well-known in scholastic lore for exact scholarship, but which originally meant a person who dwelt near a cony (rabbit) burrow. Another very scholarly name is that of Prestige, well known in the purlieus of the law and the Church. Prestige has, of course, nothing to do with worth or reputation, but comes from Prestwich in the county of Lancashire.

It is thought that many surnames come from a totally different type of place name—that is from inn signs. These signs took many forms in the days when only a minority could read and they were hung out over many businesses as well as simply inns or hostelries. Readers must recall the many occasions when in reading old romances (or imitations of them) they have encountered references to someone who abides at the sign of the painted leopard or some such description. This does not always mean an inn, but often refers to a house, similar to that of Simon the Tanner in the Street called Straight, where St Peter for a time set up his episcopal throne. It would not be hard for a man whose Christian name was Peter, and whose sign was the bell, to be called after a while, Peter Bell. Frank the goldsmith at the Rose could be Frank Rose, or at least his descendants could acquire the name Rose within a few generations. This etymology is supported by learned opinion, as against the more common form which comes from Norman Rohese. Thus there can be two sources for a name, so that the Roses of England may be noble Normans (if anything could make a Norman noble!) or just dwellers at the sign of the Rose. To resolve this little difficulty there is only one solution—genealogical research.

The various occupations took signs such as the Needle for a tailor, the Cow for a vintner, the Plow for the silkman—names which did not always denote the man's occupation, but rather his (or his wife's) fancy for a house name. From this source come many names which might easily be thought to be those of occupations.

For those who wish to study their genealogical origins, I would recommend a perusal of some simple work which deals with the tracing of ancestry. As it has been my lot for some thirty years to be intimately concerned with genealogy, I make no bones about recommending my own works on this subject. They were written originally because I found that, although I lived in the atmosphere of research and of *Burke's Peerage*, etc., I could not easily follow the books which then existed and which were aimed at helping the inquirer. Consequently, I set out to deal with the matter in an empirical way, by gathering as much data as possible and finding out for myself (and for many others) how to trace one's ancestry. My reward has lain in the receipt of letters from literally all over the world in which people have thanked me for my help and have then usually gone on to ask me some more difficult questions. In this way, I have gathered an immense amount of experience of these matters.

Trace Your Ancestors is a small work which will get the inquirer on to the right path. He can then follow this up with the larger *Your Family Tree*. Both these works are in print. Out of print, and when in print, printed in America, is the large *American Origins*. If anyone is interested in tracing his or her ancestry in countries of the continent of Europe, he or she had better try to see this work. *Your Family Tree* gives the British Isles portion of the book, but only in *American Origins* can be found a guide to genealogical sources throughout Europe.

Finally there is the matter of heraldry. This does enter into the study of surnames, and I would suggest my *Teach Yourself Heraldry (and Genealogy)*. Also the larger and more learned work, *The Story of Heraldry*, published by Country Life, Ltd.

IV. Patronymics

Nothing is commoner in the rise of surnames than to come upon a name which indicates whose son a man is. This is common form among the nations of the British Isles. The Scots have Mac meaning 'son of'—thus, in a very simple form, MacDonald, son of Donald. The Irish have the familiar 'O', as in O'Carroll or O'Callaghan, also meaning 'son of'. In Welsh the standard form was 'Ap', for 'son of', and this easy usage gave the Welshman the opportunity to carry half a dozen generations of his pedigree in a single short sentence. Ap Rice, ap Evan, ap Morice, ap Morgan, ap Llewellyn, ap Madoc, ap Meredith, ap Griffith, ap Davis, ap Owen, is a string of names which to the Saxon may seem to argue a multitude of persons, but which is merely the reiteration of 'son of'. The Normans had a similar usage in 'Fitz', so that FitzWilliam is simply 'son of William.' In connection with the latter, there is an idea that the use of Fitz before a surname, or rather as part of a surname, denotes illegitimacy. This is a mistaken view. The origin of the great house of the FitzWilliams, about whose succession there was a considerable and costly case at law some years ago, has nothing to do with illegitimacy. Their surname is an interesting example of the way in which native English families transformed themselves into imitations of the Norman conquerors. Godric, who founded this great family, was an Englishman, one of those landholders in Yorkshire who managed to survive all the vicissitudes of the Norman Conquest and its aftermath. His son was named William and married a great heiress, Aubreye de Lizour, and the grandson or great-grandson of this marriage was named FitzWilliam, a fairly early instance of the use of a surname.

The FitzWilliams are still in the peerage ranks, but during the middle ages there were many other families which bore this type of patronymic. There were the FitzAlans (Earls of Arundel and

Barons Maltravers); the FitzGeralds (Barons FitzGerald and Vesey); the famous FitzGeralds, Earls of Desmond, the last of whom died in the Tower of London and of whom Sir Bernard Burke remarks: 'The Geraldine Earls of Desmond suffered perhaps more than any other great race in Ireland the severest reverses of fortune.' There were FitzGibbons (the Earls of Clare), the Fitz-Herberts (Barons FitzHerbert), the Fitz Hughs (Barons FitzHugh), the FitzJohns (Barons FitzJohn), the FitzPatricks (Barons and Earls of Upper Ossory), the FitzPaynes (Barons FitzPayne), the FitzPiers (Earls of Essex, better known as the Mandevilles, a family which had the distinction to produce a scoundrel of the front rank, Geoffrey de Mandeville, twice made an earl by both Stephen and Matilda in the years of the Anarchy (1135–54). There were the FitzWalters (Barons F tzWalter) and the FitzWarines (Barons FitzWarine). None of these families comes from a royal bastard. Of course, there are illegitimate lines which bear the prefix Fitz. In the *Extinct Peerage* there are some cases, depending as one might perhaps expect upon King Charles II. FitzCharles, Earl of Plymouth, was one of his bastards, born of Catharine Pegg, but who died at Tangier during the siege of that city by the Moors. James FitzJames, Duke of Berwick, was a son of Charles's brother, James II, by Arabella Churchill, and became one of the ablest generals of the age. From him descend the line of the Dukes of Berwick and Alba, in the peerage of Spain. FitzRoy is the surname of the present Dukes of Grafton, the founder of this line being the second son of King Charles II by Barbara Villiers, Duchess of Cleveland. The elder son by Barbara became Duke of Southampton and also succeeded to his mother's dukedom of Cleveland, but this line died out in 1774. George FitzRoy, another son of Barbara, was made Earl and Duke of Northumberland, but he died without issue in 1716, so that his titles also became extinct. King Henry VIII contributed another of the Fitz lines to the *Extinct Peerage*, in the person of Henry FitzRoy, Duke of Richmond and Somerset, who died when he was about seventeen. At one time Henry VIII had toyed with the idea of making him legitimate, so that he could have a male heir.

At the present time, the name FitzRoy occurs in the modern *Peerage* for the families of the Duke of Grafton mentioned above, the Barons Southampton (a branch of the Dukes of Grafton), and the Viscounts Daventry (another branch from Grafton). These all

59

sprang from the *amour* of Charles II with the famous Barbara Villiers. In addition, we have FitzClarence, Earls of Munster, the offspring of William IV and Mrs Jordan, an actress. But after these there are other Fitzs who have no illegitimate connection with our past royalty, such as FitzMaurice, Earls of Orkney, and Fitz-Herbert, Barons Stafford. In short, the use of Fitz as the sign of bastard descent from royalty is merely a carrying on, or a hangover from, an old state of affairs in which the use of Fitz denoted parentage and was the equivalent of the Mac, O or Ap of other nations.

There are many families about today who bear the name of Fitz followed almost always by a Christian name. Their surnames, as may be seen by comparing them with those listed above, merely mean 'son of'—followed by whatever Christian name was used centuries ago. The use of Christian names as surnames is another side of the subject which we shall investigate later.

When we come to the ordinary English usage, the easiest form for identification purposes is the simple 'son of,' usually in the form Williamson, Jackson, Johnson and many, many others, too numerous to list. I can only select some, taking as specimens names given in the London post office telephone directory. Benson is an abbreviated form of Bennetson, or son of Bennet. Adamson is the son of Adam, a less usual form of Adams, a type which is mentioned below. Addison is said to mean son of Addy; Atkinson is a sharper form, so Dr Bardsley would affirm, of Atkins, meaning son of Atkin, or Adkin—the meaning of the latter being left in complete obscurity. There are about a third of a column of Aldersons in the directory; they are the sons of Aldred. Allanson is fairly common, though nowhere near as frequent as Anderson, or son of Andrew. Alison may be a form of Allanson (Allenson is another form) or it may have been, and more likely is, a name taken from an ancestress, thus the son of Alison, a well-known woman's name in the middle ages, and still in use today. Names were sometimes taken from the mother, in some cases because of adoption by an unmarried woman, or it may well have been because she was the stronger personality.

Robinson, Williamson, Thompson, or Thomson, Richardson, Robertson—these are names so common that no one can fail to know them, and of obvious derivation. There is another class of patronymics, where the ascription of sonship comes at the end of the name, thus Edwards, Richards, Roberts, Andrews, meaning in each case 'son of' the particular person whose Christian name is given. It is an interesting speculation how Christian names came to be used in this way, so as to denote descent, or how they stuck after several generations at the one name, instead of changing with every other generation, as in the case of the Welsh. One would have thought that the son of Richard or Richards might well have passed on to his son, not the name of the grandfather, but his own. Thus the Richards' son might well have been known as Johns or the son of John, this John having been Richard's son. This would have corresponded to the Welsh usage, where the 'ap' means simply 'son of', and thus Evan ap Griffith, ap Caradoc, ap Morgan, ap Evans merely rehearses the pedigree over some hundred to a hundred and fifty years. If put in English each generation would have as suffix -son or -s, but instead the English usage has been to take one Christian name, tack -s on to it, and leave this to denote descent over many generations. The remark on Mr Harold Wilson, that he was the fourteenth Mr Wilson, referring to the fact that Sir Alec Douglas-Home was the fourteenth Earl of Home, has considerable insight. For if we object to titles being carried on for generations, we should object to the most widespread and common of our titles, and protest against a man proclaiming his descent from the original Will, whose son some fourteen, fifteen or twenty generations back decided that the surname thus acquired should be carried on for centuries.

Some of the -son forms require a little explanation. Dawson comes from an abbreviation of David—i.e. Daw; Watson is son of Wat or Walter; Hickson or Hicks is from Hicke or Isaac. Simpson and Simson, also Sims, derive from Simm, or Simon, thus being sons of Simm or Simon. Then we have Simpkins, or Simpkinson, which are forms allied with Simkin, Simpkin, Sinkin, etc., and which are derived from the diminutive son of little Sim. Tomkins has a similar history. There are a number of names such as Colinson, Dicconson (Diccon being the nickname of Richard), Hugginson, or Hodgkinson.

A large number of names now used as surnames are simply Christian names which have been passed down, not in any form such as 'son of', Richardson or Richards, but simply and plainly as a Christian name which has become a surname. An instance of great interest is the name of Arnold, now strongly established in

English history and literature through the work of the great Dr Thomas Arnold of Rugby and his son, the poet Matthew Arnold. This name was derived from a Christian name Ernald, which is thought to be connected with the old word for an eagle, namely earn. The name soon passes from Ernald into Arnold, and then gives rise to many forms of surname, including the diminutive form, Arnott. Earn is both old German and Old English—and, in passing, Earnshaw may be noted as a surname, meaning eagle wood. Here again, as we so often find in investigating surnames and their origin, we note that there are places in England—in Nottingham, Yorkshire, and Kent—named Arnold, and the surname could have come from them, since records exist which show a person as Roger or Richard de Arnold. The only way in which the true meaning of a name which has two possible origins can be discovered is, as I have said, through genealogical research. Even then a number of cases must remain in doubt, because research cannot always tell us the first holder of the name.

A name which has no currency at all at present as a Christian name is that of Emery, yet it has had immense influence as a surname. Emerson is a name of great power in world literature, particularly that of the United States. It comes from this obscure and long overlaid Christian name, Emery. So, too, does the surname Emberson. Amory is another descendant of this font name of old England. Imray or Imrie, often found in Scotland, is also derived from it. Thus this name has its offshoots in Scotland as well as in England and the United States. In its proper form of Emery or Emory, it is still found today. What does this powerful and widespreading name mean? According to those best qualified to know, it comes from an old French (through old German) word meaning 'work-rule'. This etymology, like many others, does not convey much to us, the reason being that centuries ago the meaning of the word had gone, and those who bestowed it upon their children at baptism acted just as modern parents do, and gave the name because they liked it, and enjoyed its sound, or even perhaps because they hoped to get some favour for the child from relatives similarly named.

It is fascinating to reflect on the provenance of a little known name which has spread all over the world from its original home in Germany. But how came Christian names to become surnames? In cases where Arnold is used, to take one instance only, in the records which supply examples, names occur, such as Roger son of Ernald or Arnold. Yet there must have been many cases in which the name of Arnold came to be used for son as well as for father. Probably the neighbours, or the owner of the name himself, preferred him to be known by the name of Arnold, instead of as Richard son of Arnold. It may have been simply a question of personal preference in the first place.

As, however, Christian names have given birth in so many cases to surnames, obviously the meaning of Christian names is important. Furthermore, we have to understand that the bulk of our English Christian names are not derived from our English forbears. We have only to study any history of pre-Norman Conquest England to note that most of the names which occur in the record are unknown to us, apart from the old English documents. Alfred and Edward were too deeply imprinted in the national consciousness for any amount of Norman jack-boot methods to drive them out. Edmund, Edgar and Edith also survived, but names such as Algar, which occasionally we meet with among the upper class families of today, are conscious anachronisms. They were due to readings in the *Waverley* novels of Sir Walter Scott and other romancers, and led many of the aristocracy to give high-sounding Christian names to their children, names which they obtained from old books, under the impression that these were the names of great personages of the past, though the names, like Hereward or Ethelbert or Ethelwin, were borne by all sorts and conditions of men and women. Algar, by the way, is a surname derived from a remote period and Elgar is another form of it. It has a meaning, of 'spear', with something else added, and philologists are unable to agree as to whether it comes from Scandinavian or English, the meaning being either 'elf spear' or 'old spear', according to whether it is of Viking or English origin.

The bulk of old English Christian names did, however, pass out of use and were replaced by Norman forms. This was not unnatural, and in one instance given at the beginning of this chapter we saw the process in action. This was in the FitzWilliam family, where the pedigree begins with an old English name and soon turns to the trans-channel forms. A similar feature came in the pedigree of the Claytons of Clayton in Lancashire, where Hugh is the son of Alfgar, and thus we have a clue to the origin of this extinct family. It may have been so, too, with the Okeovers—a now

63

extinct family, but one which lasted for nearly nine centuries. The founder of the line was one Orm or Ormus Helsweyn, who was living from 1089 to 1138. He may have been, says the opening of the pedigree in *Burke's Landed Gentry*, the son of Eddulph, the Domesday tenant of Okeover. If so it would argue that this family could be of native origin. Incidentally, Orm's son was called Ralph FitzOrmus, of Okeover, but in this family the Fitz opening of the name did not remain, being replaced by the place name, Okeover, the title of the family property in Staffordshire.

One of the Christian names which survived the Norman Conquest, though mainly as a surname, was the famous Hereward, which comes from two old English words, meaning respectively 'army' and 'guard'. I say famous advisedly because of its associations with the man who was the last to offer organised resistance to the Norman conquerors, that marvellous figure of romance and history, who was known as Hereward the Wake. His parentage and his descendants are alike wrapped in mystery, but his name did not survive too far into the middle ages. It occurs up to the thirteenth century, then it shares the fate of most pre-Conquest names. However, it is now generally agreed that it gave rise to the surnames of Harward and Harwood. Some would add to these Harvard and Howard. The surname Howard has been described as rising from hogward or even from ewe herd.

In old editions of *Burke's Peerage* the pedigree of the Dukes of Norfolk began with the exploits of Hereward the Wake, giving this illustrious man as the founder of the royal and noble Howards, who stand at the head of the peers of England next to the blood royal. This passage was taken out by me, when I was Editor, on the ground that it was not proven. I do not suppose that it ever can be proved, for surely if ever there had been a family with the means of successful research to hand, it would be the Howards, whose head is the chief of the College of Arms, the principal repository of genealogical information in England? However, it is a fascinating and intriguing conjecture to think of Hereward as the founder of the line of the premier Dukes. Apart from this several notable families do contend, in the manner of the various cities that claimed to be the place of Homer's birth, to have the honour of Hereward as their founder. I was compelled to take out this assertion in the case of the Wake baronets, since I could not agree that they had proved their descent from Hereward the Wake.

Old General Harward wrote a lengthy account of Hereward the Wake, filling in the gap in an old monastic chronicler's narrative with his own conjectures. It does seem possible that a family with the name of Harwood, or Harward, is descended from the hero. Who would not want to be? After a life of adventure and battle, Hereward dies at the hands of the Normans, but not before a ring of a dozen corpses surrounds him, and with his last blow he brains the man who smites him. The Normans who slew him draw back in awe from that terrible corpse. They agreed that had England contained three such men, they would have driven William and his Normans into the sea. Charles Kingsley's romance, *Hereward the Wake*, which will always appeal to the young in heart, is based on the old chroniclers.

If Hereward is not the source of Howard, the latter is united in its origins with a group of well-known surnames—Howerd, Heward, Hewart, Huard, Huart. These appear to be derived from an old French form *huard* or 'heart brave.' It should be noted in passing that Howarth is not a case of a last consonant being altered from Howard, but of a variation of Haworth, a place name in Yorkshire; sometimes it comes from Howarth in Lancashire. Harvard is yet another variant of Hereward, so that this ancient English name has been transplanted to the United States.

Harding is a name coming from an old English word meaning 'hard'. It is found as an early rudimentary surname at the end of the twelfth century, and for a while it attracted the Norman Fitz, as in Maurice FitzHarding, a name occurring early in the pedigree of the great house of Berkeley, which in Scotland became Barclay. Sweyn was a popular name derived from the Norsemen, though it also occurs as Swan in Old English, meaning a herdsman or swine-heard. It can hardly have had this meaning when applied to the Viking chiefs who carved for themselves a kingdom out of the ruin of the tenth-century Golden Age of Saxon England. Sweyn, the father of Canute, was just before his death accepted as King of All England, and he certainly had nothing to do with herding swine. I prefer the meaning of strength, which some etymologies give to the name. In due course it became a Christian name and thence the source of our Swans, Swaynes, Swains and Swainsons.

Harold was a common name in pre-Conquest England, where it had been brought by the Danes. It was, of course, the name of the last king of pre-Conquest England, and it may have been a matter of wonder that it should have survived. Yet it did and went on to be not only a modern Christian name, but also found as a surname, in the forms Harrold, Haroll, Harald (in this form often in the Orkneys and Shetlands, where Norse influence has stayed on, and where the Scot is if anything more of a foreigner than the Englishman), Harrald and Harrod. In the last form it comes from Haroud, one of the medieval forms of the name.

Henry was a name introduced into England at the Conquest. The French pronunciation of Henry became in English Harry, so that the form Harry is not a pet form of Henry, but the correct English pronunciation, and the right form of the name in England. The Christian name gave rise to a number of surnames, such as Henryson, Harris, Harrison, Herries, Henderson and Hendry. Then there was a diminutive of the name as Hal—we remember good king Hal or bluff king Hal, meaning Henry VIII—which led to Halkin; and likewise Herriot is from the diminutive Henriot.

Searle, or Serle, is a not uncommon English surname. This is a name coming from a Christian name brought by the Normans, not from the continent, but into common use in England after the Conquest. It means (in Old English) 'armour', and must be yet another case of a word having its meaning obscured or lost, since it is hard to see why parents should call their child 'armour'. It is the source of many forms of a surname, spelt as Searle, or Serle, Serles, Searls and Serrell. Harvey, Harvie and Hervey come from an old French word meaning 'battle worthy', which seems to have more sense than the majority of such names. It was common in the middle ages as a Christian name.

Many of these Norman font names were popular in the middle ages, but dropped off at a later time, though not before they had bequeathed their quota of surnames to English. Among them we can reckon Drew, which gave rise not only to Drew as a surname, but also to Drewett, derived from the diminutive. Warin is a common name which produced a series of surnames, among them Wareing, Warring, Warring, Wearing and FitzWarin. The manor of Waring produced the Mainwarings, pronounced Mannerings.

Some of the Norman names came from a distant land and century, for the Normans, who had only a very superficial culture, were thinly disguised descendants of the Vikings. Part of the price of their settlement in Normandy had been the stipulation that they should be converted to Christianity. Some of them declined to accept baptism, and were probably known as pagans, or payens. This name stuck and was conveyed into England, where, strange to relate, it became a baptismal name and was the forerunner of some of the popular names which now figure in the annual list of *The Times*. Pain and Payne are reminders of its former widespread use.

Among the most piquant and interesting of the pedigrees embedded in the first edition of *Burke's Landed Gentry* (published in four volumes as *Burke's Commoners*) is that of the truly great and long-recorded family of Arden. This is the oldest pedigree in England, going back in unbroken male line to one Aelfwine, who had been Sheriff of Warwickshire under Edward the Confessor (1042–1066). But such a notable record was not enough for Sir Bernard Burke. He gave the pre-Conquest descent in full, and it included the great hero of romance, Guy of Warwick, still commemorated in Guy's Cliff near Warwick Castle. According to Burke, Guy won great fame at a tournament under King Ethelred II. He also gained honour all over Europe. Now the name Guy is derived from the old German *wido* meaning, possibly, 'wood'. The name did not come to England until Norman times, when it flourished greatly and was the point of departure of many surnames such as Wyatt, Wyon, Guyon, Guise and Gye. The name as a Christian name did not seem a very good choice to parents after the failure of the Gunpowder Plot in 1605. It has revived in the last hundred years and so it appears as a Christian name while its descendants, mentioned above, flourish likewise.

Gunther comes from Old German *gundhard*—'war bold' or 'hardy'. The varying surname is Gunter. Hamo, which I mentioned earlier, gave origin among other names to Hamlet, which was a variant of Hamnet, the name of Shakespeare's only son, who died at an early age. The fact that his son's name was often used as Hamlet may have predisposed the poet to an interest in the story of the Prince of Denmark, as given by the Danish historian, Saxo Grammaticus, though there the name Hamlet is derived from a quite different source, the Icelandic *amlothi*.

Gilbert and Gilbart, surnames both, are from the Christian name Gilbert, which is from old German meaning 'a bright pledge', the two constituents of the name being *gisil*, pledge, and *bertha*, bright. It has occasioned many surnames, not only the two just mentioned, but Gilbertson, Gilson and also Gibbs, Gibson, Gibbons, Gibbin, Gipps, Gilbye and Gilpin. These latter forms are

67

THE STORY OF SURNAMES

from the pet or abbreviated versions, gib or gibby. A cat was often called a gib, and it is of interest to note that our ancestors went in as much as we do for shortened versions of a name.

Godwin is one of the Old English Christian names which managed to survive the Conquest, though it was the name of King Harold's father—he was known as Harold Godwinson—and one might have expected it to go into disfavour owing to Norman arrogance and lying about the right their duke had to the throne, being thwarted by the house of Godwin. But Godwin survived and is now still found here and there as a font name. It has a numerous progeny in the surnames which it has fathered. Not only is there Godwin, but Goodwin, Godden, Goodden, Godding, Godin and Goding. Godwin comes from the compound God and wine, 'friend', whereas Goldwin is an Old English word meaning 'gold' and 'friend'. Goldwin was the origin of Goldwin, Golden, Goulden and Goulding.

Gregory, a name of great honour in the eastern church, is derived from the Greek word *gregoreo*, from *egeiro*, to be watchful. It was the name of the Pope who sent St Augustine to England in 597 to convert the English. It was a name borne by fathers of the church from a distant age and by many of the Popes. It was in use as a Christian name from the twelfth century. Many surnames come from it—Gregory itself, Gregg, Grigg, Greggs, Griggs, Gregson, Grigson and Greig.

Humphrey is used both in that form and in the other—Humphries—and comes from the French Onfroi, which itself is a version of or connection with the German Hunfrid and the Old English Hunfrith. It was the French version which caused the name to be popular in Norman England. Many surnames are connected from one source—Hugh or Hugo. They are Hugh itself, Hughes, Hugget and Huggins (the latter two are, of course, from the diminutive), while Hewes, Hewson, Hewet, Hewlett, How and Howes all come from the same source. The name Hugh means heart or mind, from Hugo in old German. Ingram is from an old German source word which can mean 'angel raven', or possibly the name of some old hero. It became in French Ingelram and so on to Ingram.

Earlier in this chapter I referred to names of women which became surnames. One of the most interesting and out of the way of these is the source of surnames such as Ibbison, Ibbetson, Ibson, Nibbs, Libby, Tibbs and Isbell. The last name gives the clue to the source. This is Isabell or Isobel, which went into many pet forms and diminutives, some of which were Ib, Nib, etc. or Ibbot.

Ives, Iveson, Ivatts, Ivetts and Ivens are the descendants in surname form of Ive, an old French name meaning perhaps yew. In England it was the Christian name of one Ivo Taillebois, one of the Norman conquerors and possibly, as Kingsley makes him out to be, a base woodcutter's son, though there is nothing necessarily base or ignoble about a woodcutter. Ivo de Taillebois married a great English lady, the sister of the unfortunate earls, Edwin and Morcar, always named together as though they were Siamese twins.

A surname flourishing to this day, only a few hundred yards from where I am writing, is Jerrome. In other forms it is simply Jerome, Jerram, Jerrems and Jarram. It is derived from a celebrated Christian name, that of the great translator of the Bible into Latin, St Jerome, who in the fourth century translated the entire Bible from Greek and Hebrew into the vulgar tongue, or Latin, hence the name given to this version, the Vulgate. It was also a famous name (before the time of St Jerome), going right back to the days of classical Greece, and to a king of Syracuse. The word comes from the Greek, *hieronumos*, meaning a sacred name.

One more example from the letter J. This is Jordan, which has given us not only Jordan, but Jordanson, Jordans, Jordison and possibly Juxon and Judd. This is, of course, derived from the chief river of the Holy Land and means in Hebrew 'flowing down'. It was much used in England as a Christian name, and it may have owed some of its popularity to the fact that many of the Crusaders must have seen the Jordan, and may even have attempted to bathe in its waters or bring some of the water home with them.

Some of the Old English names have passed almost in their ancient form right into modern times as surnames. Thus Kenrick, which in Old English would mean royal rule, is known as the surname Kendrick and also as Kenwright and Kenwrick. Leofric and Leofwin, common names before the Norman Conquest, have left their progeny of surnames. Leofric is given as the source of surnames as Leverick, Leveridge and Loveridge. The name comes from the Old English sources, leof meaning 'dear' and ric meaning 'rule'. Leofwin means 'dear friend', and from it come the names Lewin, Levin, Levinson, Livens, etc. Kenward comes from two words meaning in Old English 'brave' and 'guard'. Kenward and Kennard represent it in modern English.

Lambert, the name of a well-known family of Surrey gentry, comes from old German. It means 'bright land'. Lambart as well as Lambard, Lampert, Limbert and Lambert are the modern surnames derived from this name which probably owed its favour in medieval England to the renown of St Lambert, a Flemish saint.

Lawrence, a name of Latin origin, from the town of Laurentium, was again the name of a famous saint—he of the renowned grid iron—and it has given us the variety of surnames clustered around Lawrence, namely Laurence, Lawrenson, Lawrie, Laurie, Lawson, Larry, Lowson, Larkin and others. In all these cases, where a name has many seemingly unconnected forms, it is due to the constant abbreviation of names, and to pet forms, as well as to possibly derisive forms.

Leonard gives us Lenard and Lennard, meaning 'lion hardy'. Lewis or Louis is, of course, a French personal name, for long of immense popularity in France, whence it came to England. It has given us the surnames of Lewis, Lowis, Lewse and Lewison, though the form Lewes can come from the place in Sussex. Lyall, Lyell, etc. may be from the personal name Lionel. Lovell, which in the late eighteenth and early nineteenth centuries was a name of popular romance, is supposed to be derived from an Anglo-French name, Love meaning, of all things, 'wolf'. Lowell and Lovat are other forms which this name assumed. Luke, the name of the evangelist and beloved physician, gave rise to many surnames such as Luke, Lucas and diminutive forms such as Luckett, Lucock, Lukin and Luckin.

It would be easy, but tedious, to run through the whole alphabet of names which have come from Christian names. Some are of special interest. Magnus is a name which was frequently used in Norway in the middle ages, probably because Magnus I, King of Norway, was so christened. His father was asleep at the time of his birth, and as baptism had to be given quickly, the responsible priest thought it best to stand well with the king by calling his son, 'great'. It has caused the surnames Magnus, Manson and Magnusson.

Miles is a Christian name often found in the middle ages in England. It is not clear what is the exact meaning of the word, which is often rendered in documents in medieval times as Milo. It could be from *miles*, a soldier. An instance is cited of a fishmonger who had adopted as his surname the Christian name, Miles, of his feudal lord. Miles, Mills and Milson are the modern representatives among our surnames.

Neil is a fairly common surname, along with Neal and Nielson. They derive from Nigel, or Neil or Niall, which comes, so it is thought, from an Irish root, meaning 'champion', but when latinised it was thought to be a variant or diminutive of *niger*, 'black'. Philip, which means a 'lover of horses', has given many names to our list. There are Philips, Philipson, Philps, Phelips, Phelps, Philpot, Philcox, etc. Randal again has passed into numerous forms—Randall itself, Rand, Ranson and Rankin. The original of the name is Randwulf, from two words meaning 'shield' and 'wolf'. Many of the medieval Christian names are curious to us. For example Saer or Sayer, as Christian names, have passed away, yet left us the heritage of Sayer as a surname.

Walter, Walters, Watkin and Watson are from Walter and its slang form, Wat. William has, of course, given to us a large number of surnames—from Williams to Willings or Willis.

Sometimes surnames have a habit of coming back as Christian names. Leslie is an example in point. It is a Scottish place name, but towards the end of the nineteenth century it became popular in England (also as Lesley) as a Christian name and has not decreased in use since then.

The habit of using surnames as Christian names arose after the Reformation. It may have had something to do with the desire to weld estates together through family alliances. The name of Lord Guildford Dudley, son of the infamous Duke of Northumberland and husband of Lady Jane Grey, is a well-known example. It may well have been the forerunner of many of those hyphenated surnames which from the eighteenth century were the hall mark of aristocracy and the sign that a union of estates had taken place. The use of surnames as Christian names may have been an earlier attempt to represent this.

From the few examples which I have given it may be seen how many of our surnames come from the father's name, either in straight patronymics, or in the form of a Christian name, which may have come down the ages unchanged, or strangely transformed so that without special study it is impossible to recognise its parentage.

From local names, and from patronymics, have come a huge quantity of our names. It has to be remembered also that many of the place names are in their origin names of persons.

V. Names from Occupations

Many surnames come from occupations once practised by an ancestor. It often happened in past days that for several generations son succeeded father in a craft, and so it was natural for a family to acquire a name from the occupation which had been their liveli-hood. The biographer of the great Sir Edward Marshall Hall, Edward Marjoribanks, tells us that even in the nineteenth century, the various families of Hall in the district where the famous lawyer was born were distinguished by terms derived from their trade or profession; there were lawyer Halls and butcher Halls and so on. In Sir Walter Scott's novel *The Fair Maid of Perth*, the family of the Glover is known by that name in the fourteenth century, being an incipient surname. Much more so was this the case when surnames were in the making. All of us can think not only of Glovers, but of Tailors, Butchers, Sadlers, Cooks, Butlers, Bakers and many more.

At the very beginning we have to distinguish between surnames which have been taken from an office and those which have come from a trade. The reason for this is that in the middle ages the offices of attending upon the monarch were claimed by the greatest nobles. Thus we have the surname of Butler, that of the Marquess of Ormonde, whose arms show three covered cups, emblematic of the fact that the Marquess is the Hereditary Chief Butler of Ireland. The surname was clearly taken from the appointment of Theobald FitzWalter as Chief Butler by Henry II. This FitzWalter was the descendant of a Norman adventurer who had come into England at the time of the Conquest, and he had accompanied Henry II into Ireland after it had been conquered by Strongbow. The office of Chief Butler consisted more in the arrangements for serving the King's wine rather than in the actual wine pouring, though on state occasions of great importance it was customary for a great noble to perform one or two actual pourings himself.

72

Another personage of even greater importance than the Chief Butler was the Marshal, who undertook to arrange the marshalling of the guests and to look after the chief functions of the royal household. The head of the British peerage is the Earl Marshal, the Duke of Norfolk. At a date much earlier than the bestowal of this office upon the house of Howard, there was a family named Marshal which derived its surname from the holding of the office. These were the Barons Marshal, whose surname was at first spelt Mareschall. Henry II conferred the office of Marshal upon the then head of this family, which became extinct in the male line in the year 1316.

In Scotland there was also a family which had the position of Earl Marshal (in Scots, Marischal), but the office in their case gave them their title, as Earls Marischal, while they retained their surname Keith, derived from a place in Banffshire. Then, in addition to these examples, we have the illustrious name of Stuart or Stewart, which as I mentioned in Chapter I comes from the office of High Steward to the Crown of Scotland. In this instance we see how a family, which once held the office, however great, of a household appointment, eventually succeeded to the throne itself.

It should be realised, of course, that not all those who bear the name of Butler, Marshal or Stewart are necessarily descended from the great nobility. There were many butlers, many marshals and many stewards. The last-named in some cases was the sty-ward or man who looked after the pig sties. In olden days there were many more domestics than are likely ever to be found again in the world. Service was the recognised form of employment for multitudes, who would otherwise have been without work. Nor were servants always to be pitied. The annals of the great houses of the past contain many examples of the overbearing insolence of servants, who because they realised completely their own inequality with their masters, were often wont to give them advice and to attend to matters in the family as though it were their own. The identification of the servant with his master or mistress sometimes led them, as I conjectured in the previous chapter, to adopt the family name for a surname. I think that this practice may well account for the widespread existence of some otherwise aristocratic surnames. There is a case in Ireland where a boy who had been working in the house of a great family, and was known as O'Callaghan's Corney, eventually succeeded in buying the property after the death of the last male and adopted the name. There must have been many such cases, otherwise how can one account for the widespread use of such names as Courtenay, often spelt somewhat differently but none the less the same name, or of Burke, as aristocratic a name as one could wish for (coming from De Burgo), but now very common in Ireland?

Spencer or Spenser is a fairly common name, but some of the earlier bearers of it belonged to the higher echelons of society, for a spencer was a butler or steward and the Spencer, whose surname is commemorated in the full name of Sir Winston Spencer Churchill, was not an underling. Here again, however, there were many spencers or spensers (despensers as the name was originally spelt) whose connection with royalty or the court was not proven.

When we hear of the Lord Great Chamberlain or the Lord Chamberlain, we are inclined to think of anyone with the surname of Chamberlain as being of noble lineage, especially as we consider that this family has produced three notable politicians within the last hundred years, one of whom became Prime Minister. In tact, the title of chamberlain was as common as that of butler. In *Henry IV*, Part I, there is a reference to the chamberlain of the inn, whose guests Falstaff and Prince Hal are about to rob. This gives us the measure of the position of chamberlain in the majority of cases. The man was the official or servant of an inn who showed the guests to their rooms or, at most, who arranged where they were to sleep. Stepping a little higher we have the chamberlain of a noble household, whose office is still discharged by the butler of the few great houses which can yet afford to keep one.

Most of us would understand the meaning of a name like Sheriff, which should be derived from the Shire-reeve, or Sheriff, whose jurisdiction was so firmly established that not even the Norman Conquest was able to overthrow it and replace it with a foreign term. But what of names like King, Pope, Abbot or Duke? Do we really mean that these names came from someone who held the position indicated by the name? In fact, such names border rather upon nicknames, which I shall consider in the next chapter. They were given, no doubt, for the reason that the person concerned appeared to have kingly qualities or faults, or else because he was a skilled performer in the numerous mystery plays of the middle ages. Clearly, when the clergy were arranging these plays, they would want good actors, and anyone who has seen a performance of the

74

Wakefield Cycle will know that the histrionic ability required is of no mean order. Consequently, someone who could play Herod of Jewry, or a Roman Emperor, or the Pharaoh of Egypt would be likely to be signalled out and spoken of, not with ridicule, but with great respect. Duke, of course, may mean simply, as in its original Latin *dux*, leader and hence may denote no more than the possession of a leading position in the small community in which the owner of the name lived.

Sometimes a name survives to show what was once the prevalence of the word. Thus Dempster is another form of deemster, or judge, which was a native term in the north and is still in the Isle of Man, but which has been displaced in favour of judge or justice in ordinary usage in English.

Even more peculiar than the survival of certain names, or the form in which they are found, is the fact that some terms from occupations have not lived on at all. We have no Grocers, though Groser, meaning a wholesaler, is sometimes found. In the middle ages, there were many persons entered on nominal rolls as gaolers, but the name only just survives in the forms Galer, Gayler or Jailler. Anyone who looks down the list of occupations and professions listed in Chaucer's *Canterbury Tales* will wonder why so many are not represented in our language today. Where is the Summoner? Where the Lawyer? True, Lawman is with us, but one would have thought that a profession so ancient and of such importance as that of the law would have had more representation among our surnames. Contrast its absence with the numerous Parsons (meaning a servant of the parson) or Reeves.

Possibly the most extraordinary surname, which is accepted by everyone without question, is that of Smith. There are said to be 200,000 separate families of Smith in England at present. Of these the overwhelming majority take their surname from their ancestor's occupation—workers at the smithy. I believe I am right in saying that only one family of Smith comes from a source other than that of the trade. That is the family of Smeeth, the name of two places, one in Norfolk, the other in Kent. Why this preponderance of Smith as a surname over all other trades? Was the smith a person of such local importance, and was he always the man of personality in the village, like Longfellow's blacksmith? Or like Harry Gow, or Smith, in Scott's *Fair Maid of Perth*?

Dr Bardsley gives an attempted explanation, which is ingenious.

75

It is that smith covered a multitude of occupations, such as gold-smith, tinsmith, etc. But if that were the case, the survival of gold-smith, arrowsmith, etc. would have done away with the simple un-qualified smith. To make the matter more curious, in a tenth century work, the *Homilies* of Abbot Aelfric, the smith, though referred to with some respect, did not come high in the list of occupations mentioned. Is the explanation to be found in the long periods of war which make up the history of medieval England? When the sovereign was liable at any time to call out his subjects for distant campaigns, did not the position of the smith assume a greater importance than ever before? Did not his become the master undertaking in a village? The knight or squire required the services of someone who could fit him out for the wars. He found this man in the local smith or armourer of his native village, and the craft of the latter responded in time to the importance given to it. The smith's craft took on an importance which is reflected in the vast number of those who bear the name today. Just to add that little touch of snobbery which makes England what it is, we have a Latin translation, Faber. We should add that some Fabers do not come from the anvil, but from a Christian name which has become a surname.

Some surnames of office have persisted from early times, but with shades of meaning which have varied a good deal. Alderman calls up the picture of a holder of civic office, from the Old English ealdormann, which meant the head of a guild, but was also used in pre-Conquest days for a nobleman, a lord. It lost its signification of nobility owing to the adoption of earl, from Old English eorl, used in imitation of the jarl or noble leader of the Viking hordes. In its turn Earl has appeared as a surname in English, along with many variants—Harle, Hearl, Hurl, Hurle, etc.—and it is said that these names are derived from the lofty or noble habits and outlook of an ancestor, in short a nickname, or else, as mentioned above, from the ability to act in a pageant or mystery play.

Many names of apparent office come, in fact, into the section of nicknames, which we shall discuss later, but they can be briefly mentioned here: such are Cardinal, Canon, Deacon, Pope, Priest, King, etc.

The list of the London Livery Companies furnishes an interest-ing commentary on the survival or departure of surnames. The two leading companies are the Mercers and the Grocers. The latter have been sparing in their gift of names to posterity; the former have given us Mercer, Mercier and Merchiers. Yet considering the extensive sway of these trades, and the fact that in essentials they have lived unto this day, it is curious that they should have not produced a large progeny, especially considering the enormous extension of Smith.

Some trades have left names which have outlived the occupation itself. Thus we have the Worshipful Company of Loriners, which gave rise to Lorimer, Lorrimar and Loriner. These were the spurriers, whose trade passed into limbo with the decay in provision of spurs. Bowyers have lived on in their nominal descendants, yet their trade has gone out far more quickly than anything connected with horsemanship. Shoemaker (with variants, Shoemake and Schoemaker) has lived, but of Cordwainer there is no more trace than of the trade so named. Paver, Pavier, Pavior, Paviour and Pavyer show their paternity from the pavior, whose livery company still exists.

One remembers that John Milton's father was a scrivener, and many persons were so named from this trade, which meant the craft of one who writes books or copies manuscripts and which had a connection with the law. Scriven, Scrivens, Scrivings and Scrivenor come from this source. The most curious feature of this list is that many names of trades which are common to this day are not represented in the surname nomenclature. The fishmongers, the shipwrights, haberdashers, ironmongers, gunmakers are with us, very much so indeed, yet where are the surnames derived from their occupations?

Looking down the list, many surnames are readily accounted for: goldsmith, skinner, vintner (in the form, vinter or vintiner), taylor, salter, brasier, baker, barber, brewer, butcher, carpenter, cook, cooper, cutler, dyer, fletcher (the maker or seller of arrows), gardener, glover, horner (another name which has outlived its trade at least in the medieval form), mason, painter, plumber (plummer in later and more aristocratic usage), sadler, turner, tyler, weaver. But why only these, and not clothworker, apothecary, basketmaker, clockmaker, coachmaker, distiller, fanmaker, feltmaker, knitter, girdler, innholder, muscian, and many more which have not conferred on their practitioners any form of surnominal immortality.

We find the name Carman, but this is not thought to have any connection with the trade of a carman, but is said to come from old Norse, meaning a male or adult male.

It is usually impossible for the modern descendant of one of these long dead office holders or practitioners of a trade, to discover the first person of his line who bore the name. The modern investigator is left with something more precious by far than an exact pedigree, for he can fill in the remaining portion of his lineage by using his imagination. Suppose someone to be named Panther, or Panter. He or she is descended from the panter or paneter who had the charge of the pantry in the household of a notable person. After having traced the ancestry into the limits set by the parish registers, which began in 1538, you can set your imagination to work. Going back in your pedigree to about 1600, you will have to think over the two centuries between that date and about 1400, when surnames were beginning to stick. You can imagine your ancestor going about his duties with a high seriousness, seeing to it that his employer was not cheated by the under servants or by his suppliers. Who was his lord? We cannot tell, but it is open to you to think of your ancestor at twenty removes looking after the buttery or store in a great castle—who can tell, perhaps in that of John of Gaunt or even of the King himself. From time to time he might receive a word of commendation from his lord; we hope that there were no distressing scenes similar to those in the history of Pharaoh's servants who told their dreams to Joseph.

Yes, observe this shadowy figure well; but for his successful management of the store, you would never be here. That goes, of course, for all of us. We are the descendants of the fittest to survive, those tough men and women who could outlive the Black Death, the horrors of medieval surgery and medicine, and the civil wars and foreign expeditions of England's history.

Another domestic who would have an important part to play in a great household was the sewer, whose name survives in that form. It may be derived also from a French word meaning shoemaker, but the more frequent origin is from the domestic who arranged the tables and set the dishes, as well as serving many of them. Seneschall or Senskell comes from the seneschal or steward, a major-domo in fact. Thinking over the names of offices which formerly existed in the households of the nobility, one is driven to the conclusion that the serving of a meal must have been an uncommonly protracted affair, with so many officers to see to its supervision. It was important, too, that the food should be tasted to ensure that it was not poisoned. So there were assayers, or says, hence in some cases (not all, for there were some whose name came from the great family of Saye) names which survive in the origins of Saye or Sayer. The Spooner makes his own etymology clear, but as some writers have remarked there were no Forkers, if only because forks were a comparatively late invention, and by the end of the sixteenth century names were not so likely to be derived from an occupation. Carver could be a carver in the medieval household, but is more often derived from the carving of stone or wood.

One of the most distinguished names in Scottish history is that of Napier. The family used to wish to derive their name from an ancestor who said that he was 'na peer'—in Scots, that is, when he was fleeing in disguise from his enemies, but in many cases it must have come from the naperer, or man who attended to the table-cloths. In early times it was the name given to the official who attended upon the sovereign's table, hence its early use by noble Normans, some of whom emigrated to Scotland, to answer the call of David the Saint, a king who decided to staff his kingdom with more able persons, English and Norman, than he could find in Scotland itself.

Sometimes an occupational name has occasioned a confusion in genealogy. Take the case of Grosvenor, one of the most renowned names in the British aristocracy today. Its derivation is from *le gros venour,* or chief huntsman, and a great legend or rather myth (for no evidence has yet been discovered for the story) has been built upon this foundation. It has been said that in Normandy there was the office of Great Hunter to the Duke, and that the person who held this office derived his surname from it, and also that on accompanying the Duke in his expedition against England in 1066, he held both surname and office, and that these have been perpetuated in the family of the Dukes of Westminster. Unfortunately, careful investigation and research have not borne out this interesting story. Grosvenor is from chief or great hunter, but the office of such is still to be discovered, lost no doubt in the forests of Normandy or the vaster forests of conquered England.

Many common names are explainable on the hypothesis of occupation as their source. Page is such a one; there must have been thousands of pages in the middle ages in England, because this was the accepted way for a youth of good family to advance to knight-

79

hood. So, too, we expect to find plenty of knights. They were the backbone of the medieval army, until in the fourteenth century the bowman took over from them, with disastrous results to the chivalry of France and Scotland. The history of the word knight is an enlightening commentary on the outlook of our forefathers. Of course, there were personal fighting men around the kings and great lords of pre-Conquest England, and Charles Kingsley was not wrong when he referred to the knights of Hereward and to English forms of knighthood. The term knight, however, comes from an English word, *cniht*, a servant, youth or boy. Just as we refer to some ghastly hooligans, or savage denizens of our former colonies, as boys—'what are the boys doing tonight'—so the post-Conquest English said much the same about the beef-fed rascals who were gaining land and money at the Conqueror's behest and at the expense of Englishmen. It was only gradually, under the influence of the Church, that the 'boys' became the stalwart guardians of the peace and the valiant heroes of the Crusades.

Squireship was another step to knighthood, and here we come upon one of the terms which, used as a surname, is easily explained, but which in ordinary usage requires an erudite elucidation. Squire, Squires and Squier are from the Middle English *escuyer*, or shield-bearer. The duties of the squire were to attend upon the knight and to be faithful and loyal to him whatever the odds. His duties also included the care of his lord's armour and assistance with his weapons in the hour of battle. How, then, did this term become the common esquire of today, beloved of every mail order writer and slick salesman in print? The answer is that esquire is a rank, the last but one in the table of precedence which was drawn up in the reign of Henry VIII and which is still valid today. Many persons who aspired to knighthood did not always attain this onerous distinction, which entailed, among other things, the first place in battle and the most eminent post of danger. These 'failed' knights, to use an Indian expression, did not, of course, lose gentility by failure to gain the golden spurs. They constituted a rank of gentlemen, and as such were always expected to be armigerous and to have a fair estate in land. To this day the creation of esquires is continued by Her Majesty, for when she grants a coat of arms to anyone, he automatically becomes esquire.

The fighting man, who won the great battles of Crécy, Poitiers, Agincourt, Hamildon Hill, Falkirk, Flodden and Navaretta, was the archer. He has left behind him the familiar Archer, the not so well-known Larcher, or L'Archer, and of course the Bowman. The bowyer and the fletcher, already mentioned, were the gunmakers, so to speak, of the time and they have just as naturally as the warrior left their mark on our surnames. Boyer is another form of bowyer.

Medieval battle contributed many names which have outlived their original occasions. Scrymgeour or Scrimgeour belongs here and is the surname of a famous family in Scotland, that of the Earl of Dundee. For many ages this noble family has had the privilege of carrying the standard of Scotland. Latterly it has become an honour that comes to life only at coronations. The definition of the name gives it as coming from a fencing expert or master, but this does not suit the history of the family in question. They give as its meaning the term 'hardy warrior'. Long ago, in the thirteenth century, before the Scrymgeours attained to this privilege, the name of the family which had the honour of bearing the standard was Bannerman. The representative of this family sent me his pedigree when I was compiling the *Landed Gentry*, and it appears that the family have cherished the memory of their lost hereditary honour for over six hundred years.

Many names connected, apparently, with war must have lost their significance by the time they became regular surnames. Thus Gunn, or Gun or Gunns comes from a root, Gunn, which in old Norse is 'battle'. Someone must at some time have acquired this surname and then the name must have passed on, without the original meaning being properly understood. It would seem that this is a personal name which became a surname rather than an occupational name. It should, however, be observed that the present Lord Lyon, Sir Thomas Innes of Learney, in his book, *Clans, Septs and Regiments of the Highlands of Scotland* (page 224), while remarking that the Gunns are of Norse origin, adds: 'The Gunns were a warlike clan of Caithness and Sutherland.' So perhaps the name was not ill-bestowed or obtained.

An unusual name is that of Juster or Jewster. It comes from the word jouster, or fighter at a tournament. Here again, as with the conception of knighthood, there was a great development from the early days of the tournament. In the rules of the tourney the loser had to give up his armour and horse to the winner. Harsh and ungentlemanly practices were very common in the joust of the earlier middle ages. The chivalrous habits of later times came into being only very gradually. The courtesy of the Black Prince would have been unknown or unappreciated in the tough and brutal days of his great-great-grandfather. The knights of the time of Edward I, or Richard Coeur de Lion, were capable of plenty of 'smart Yankee tricks', their object being the same as that of our transatlantic cousins, or not so near cousins—frankly, to win.

Back to the house or castle of those times. The ladies had their own apartment, and the post of bowerman was very important. He was not an eunuch on the lines of the eastern seraglio, but it was up to him to guard his lord's honour, or to be ready, according to his temperament or outlook, to shut his eyes for a consideration. No wonder he has left some legacies behind him in the realm of our names. Not only Bowerman in its plain and simple form, but also the—at first sight—less clear forms of Boorman, Borman or Burman. Then, too, there are Bowra, Bowrah, Boarer, Boorer, Borer and Burra. Clearly the positions of guardian of the ladies' bower must have been both numerous and important.

Bond is derived, so we are told, from the bondman, or serf, whose lowly status persisted right up to the close of the middle ages in England. There are other forms, which give us Bonds, Bondy, Bound, Bounds, Bundy, etc. This is not a very complimentary origin for some of the families of gentry which bear it. There it is, however, and some families take a very proper pride in the achievements of the ancestor who rose from his lowly station and made his descendants what they are. Thus the Elmhirsts of Elmhirst in Yorkshire begin their pedigree with one Robert, a serf who lived and died *circa* 1300–1360 on the land which his descendants still own, but whose son became a freeman.

In the history of England many families of the greatest rank have sunk from their high estate and their places have been taken by the descendants of others whom the once mighty would scarcely have deigned to notice.

Clark and Clerk, Clarkson, etc. are numerous names and take their origin from a very honourable occupation. In the list of England's kings one, Henry I (1100–1135), bears the nickname Beauclerk, or fine scholar. How far his scholarship had advanced beyond the rudiments of reading and writing we are not sure. But to be a clerk or a cleric in those days meant to be an educated man. Considerable time and pains were necessary to the attainment of this status.

There were large numbers of clerics, who for the sake of their careers were in minor orders, which did not entail any rigid departure from the world. It may be recalled that Thomas á Becket, or St Thomas of Canterbury, was in very minor orders when the exigencies of his friend the king (Henry II) forced him into the See of Canterbury and necessitated his ordination as deacon and priest and consecration as bishop in the same day. Becket was then a clerk, and many of these clerks did not proceed to full orders and celibacy. Hence their numerous descendants and the down-grading of the name to denote a lower class of clerical worker. Clerk in Holy Orders does, of course, preserve the old meaning.

Names from occupations are almost endless and are often obscured in their meaning from the manner in which words have developed. Thus Card and Carder are the same in origin and denote one who cards wool. Carter is easier to explain, because we have not yet lost the idea of a carter as of one who drives a cart and probably carries goods from place to place, though the almost universal substitution of the motor-driven vehicle for the horse-drawn will perhaps soon render the word out of date. Cartwright is, of course, the wright or maker of carts. Blader is a name which might very easily escape in the search for meaning; it denotes a blader or maker of blades.

Many names, now borne by aristocratic families, betray by their etymology the fact, understandable enough, that the family in question has risen from lowly origin. The Cokes of Norfolk have been a notable family for four hundred years. Their surname is, however, the same as that of Cook, and is pronounced like that. This will explain why the ancestry of the Earls of Leicester goes back only three generations before the famous Sir Edward Coke, the noted lawyer of the reigns of Elizabeth I and James I. Smith, again, the frequency of which name has already been remarked, is borne as surname by five peerage families—those of Birkenhead, Hambledon, Bicester, Colwyn and Dudley—and by the baronetcy family of Smith-Marriott. Stuart is the surname of the Earls Castle Stewart, which is a branch of the royal Stuarts, or the family of the High Steward. Taylor is the patronymic of the Marquess of Headfort and of Lord Grantchester. Ward, the surname of the Viscounts Bangor and the Earls of Dudley, is derived from an ancestor who was a guardian or watchman, which perhaps explains why the family's pedigree does not go back before the

83

sixteenth century; they were not of great importance before that time.

Vyner, a surname in the Marquess of Northampton's family, is what one would expect it to mean, a vine dresser. Roper, the surname of Lord Teynham, is from the occupation of a long past ancestor who made ropes. Paget, the name of the Marquess of Anglesey, is a diminutive of page. Parsons may well mean one who worked or lived at the parson's or priest's house, or worked for him; it is the surname of the Earls of Rosse. Proctor, or Prockter, is derived from a word in Middle English which meant a manager or agent, especially in a church court. It is now part of the surname of a baronet. Mason is the surname of Lord Blackford. A very ancient occupational name is that of Forester, which is borne by a family (the Lords Forester) whose ancestors are traceable as foresters in the early twelfth century. They were then holding custody of part of the Wrekin Forest in Shropshire. A collier is the maker or seller of charcoal, and the name Collier is borne by the family of Lord Monkswell. Tanner is another example of a surname which requires no explanation. Coates can mean the dweller by the cote or cottage, or shelter, but it also means one who lives at the cottage or one who was employed to look after the sheepcote.

Then there is the curious surname of the Marquesses of Bath—Thynne. This would naturally suggest a nickname origin, from a slender or meagre ancestor. Contrary to this, the Thynnes say that one of their ancestors in the sixteenth century lived at an inn, or a place called The Inn, and thus arose the family name, from the description of John or William at the Inne, corrupted or slurred into Thynne. The family's name was originally Boteville, and it seems likely that one of the more prosperous sixteenth-century forebears was a successful innkeeper, in which case the name is occupational.

The list of occupational surnames can be exhausted only when everyone's curiosity about his or her own surname is satisfied, which will probably be never. It would be impossible to go over all the names which have been derived from the work of an ancestor. It can be suggested, however, that anyone whose surname does suppose an occupational origin should seriously consider that this is the correct explanation.

The contrary view point was held by a client of mine, many years ago, who called upon me in high seriousness to ask me to trace his ancestry. He told me of an encouraging fact, that his fore-bears were strewed in their graves around the hamlet where they had lived for some centuries, but that he would like them to be (metaphorically) disinterred and examined, so that the full length of his pedigree could be drawn out. I accordingly got to work and soon found plenty of generations which could be set forth in orderly fashion. After about five of them had been duly catalogued, I lighted upon an ancestor who had been set down in my client's loose notes as—the form given here is, of course, fictitious—John Butcher Horwell. When I examined the parish registers of the district, I found that John Horwell was correct, but that the Butcher part of the name was indeed not a name at all, only that of John Horwell's occupation. I set out the facts in my current report, but write as often as I liked, I never heard any more of my client. He had had enough of the fact that his ancestor had been a trades-man, a butcher.

Snobbery at the origin of names will rear its head again and again, but it is useless. The facts of ancestry cannot be altered, even if some of the Tudor bigwigs did forge documents in order to prove to others, if not to themselves, that they were of Norman origin.

Tracing one's surname can be as fascinating as tracing one's ancestry, with which it is bound up. Couchers can enjoy the thought that some long dead predecessor did make couches and was an upholsterer; similar in origin is Couchman. The great modern family of Colman, for so many generations resident in Norfolk, originated in a charcoal burner, relic of the days when the south of England was the centre of the iron industry of this country. Fidler played on the fiddle, perhaps singing for his supper. Fitter may mean either carpenter or one who helped to fit out ships and to load them with their cargoes. Seward can be either sow herd or keeper of pigs, in short a Gurth, as described in *Ivanhoe;* or it can be derived from Old English and mean victory-lord. You must take your choice. There are enough rules to guide anyone.

VI. Nicknames

On the subject of original nicknames, Mr Harry Pirie Gordon, editor of *Burke's Landed Gentry* in 1937, once remarked that 'the founders of Norman families were not always either Norman or noble, and the nice ears of some of the descendants, even of the best of them, have at times been shocked at the impoliteness of the original nicknames applied to ancestors who would themselves have smiled to see the polite development during later centuries of the Norman equivalent of "Fat-Chaps" or "Big-Belly", into the respected nomenclature of today'. In this connection it should be remembered that in the roll of our kings from William the Conqueror to Richard III there are no surnames as such. The nicknames bestowed on these sovereigns are indicative of the type of nickname given to their subjects, with this difference that sometimes the latter slang names stuck. William I himself is always styled either the Conqueror or the Bastard. William II was Rufus or the red-haired. Henry I was Beauclerk, or fine scholar. With Stephen we come upon the place name, he being styled of Blois. Henry II was named of Anjou; Richard I bore the nickname of Coeur-de-Lion; John was Lackland; Henry III was of Winchester; Edward I was Longshanks, he being six feet two inches in height. Edward II was of Carnarvon; Edward III of Windsor; Richard II, his grandson, was of Bordeaux—these names being of the sovereign's birthplace. Richard's father was the famous Black Prince, so called from the colour of his armour. Henry IV was known as Bolingbroke or of Lancester; Henry V was Harry of Monmouth; Henry VI seems to have had no pet name or derisory adjective; perhaps his sanctity of character held men back. Edward IV was of York; so, too, was the boy king Edward V; but with the last of the Plantaganets—Richard III—we come upon a genuine nickname, Crouchback. After this, in passing to the Tudors, we begin royal surnames.

86

There is no doubt that some surnames are derived from nicknames, though, as I have pointed out earlier, if the nickname was
pejorative in character, the descendants would surely have tried to
shake it off. Admittedly this is not easy, as anyone who has ever
had the misfortune to acquire an unpleasant nickname can testify.
Perhaps an illustration taken from names of parties or sects may
help. Tory is a name which excites great indignation among the
opponents of the Conservative party; at least they use Tory as an
epithet of attack. Yet numerous Conservatives rejoice to call themselves Tories and glory in the name, though, as Lord Macaulay
long ago pointed out, the origin of the term was in the name given
to some Irish robbers. Similarly, the older enemies of the Tories
were dubbed Whigs, a name which came from a Scottish sect
which suffered great persecution from the government in the
seventeenth century. Yet it was used by even so distinguished a
thinker as Edmund Burke with approval when he remarked that
he was a good Whig.

In our own time in England, the old term of abuse, Papist, is
now used by some converts to Catholicism as though it were an
adjective of admiration or approval. Quaker is certainly not now a
term of abuse, though it has never been the official name of the
Society of Friends. Few members of the Society would disapprove
of being called Quakers. Radical was once an insulting word, but
modern Liberals like to refer to their party as being the radical
alternative to Socialism.

So, too, it must have been with many nicknames. Perhaps after
a while they lost their unpleasant meaning and became obscured,
so that the bearers were pleased with the terms. This must have
been the case with the great name of Scrope, which is said to mean
'crab', applied no doubt, as I said in Chapter 1, to the gait or walk
of an ancestor, but which in its passage from Scandinavia, via
Normandy, to England had the original meaning slurred over.
Many of the medieval names have gone, if only for the reason that
they were the product of a time which was extremely coarse and
cruel. Few nicknames are pleasant, or kindly, since they would
not be bestowed if people had consideration for the feelings of
others, or were not addicted to sarcasm.

There are, it is true, surnames derived from nicknames of convenience as they may be termed. Thus we have Uncle as a surname,
which Dr Bardsley thought (erroneously) to be obsolete. He con-

sidered it to have its present meaning when conferred, so that we find in old records references to William le Huncle or John le Uncle. In Old English the word for uncle was eam or (later) eme, and this is the origin of Eames. Ames, on the other hand, comes from a version of *amicus*, the Latin for friend, which was used of persons of lower degree. Cousins is a fairly common surname and derives from someone called le Cuseyn. Kinsman is the same in origin, coming from words denoting kinship. There must have been at times great confusion when one thinks of the enormous number of persons who would have borne such surnames.

Widdowson is another case of a distinguishing name which was given by neighbours and the like to mark out a man from his fellows. Faderless was found in former times and carries its meaning on its syllables. Fathers is a much more unlikely name, considering the fact of its meaning, yet it may have come from some spiritual relationship, that possibly between a pupil and master or religious man. Brothers may refer to members of some society or brotherhood. Brotherson needs no explanation. Neve is the Norman French for nephew. Frere is a French form of brother, and the motto of the famous Frere family, *Frère aime frère*, is a play on its meaning. Parent may be another of these nicknames derived from family circumstances.

Wealth and poverty gave rise to many names. Poore seems an obvious case in point, but may not always be derived from the person's condition. It often appears as Power, or Powers, and for this reason may not always be from old French *povre*, meaning poor, but is perhaps cognate in origin with the name Poer, as in Le Poer Trench, or in the surname of Edgar Allan Poe, whose forbears were said to be members of the famous Irish family of Poer. Rich speaks for itself in the majority of instances, though it is said that it means also 'dweller by the stream.' Lepper would give us a meaning of a very unpleasant nature, but it may sometimes be concealed under Leaper, which might be derived from a leaper or dancer. The medieval leper was a most unfortunate creature; as no cure was then known for his disease, he was shunned by all and compelled to live in dreadful solitude. One must not jump to conclusions, for Ragg does not denote a poverty-stricken condition, but comes from an old Danish name Wragi.

Coming to names drawn from the physical shape of the body and its characteristics, there is naturally a vast field. Lust is short no doubt for Lusty, and we have numerous Strong men, Long men, and Short men, even a Longfellow, whose name has become familiar because of the poet. Bigg, Little, Lowe, Thin and Stout (the latter referring to courage and sturdy behaviour), Young, Old, Older, etc. all carry their meaning fairly clear about them, though Stout may have a mental rather than a physical signification. The enumeration of these names can be made by almost anyone, but we also have Shorter, Younger, Littler, Senior, Elder, Grose (French for large), Grant (i.e. grand or large), Petty or Pettit, Twist, Strongitharm, Youngman, Wightman (said to mean a strong man or wight).

Many parts of the human frame were used to provide surnames. Thus Cheke, meaning a jaw bone (an ancestor was perhaps possessed of a prominent jaw bone), which became the surname of Sir John Cheke, who in Milton's verse, 'taught'st Cambridge and King Edward Greek'. In this connection I must interject the fact that Jowett, the name borne by the famous Master of Balliol, in the latter part of the last century, is said to be derived from a pet-name, Jouet. How strange would this have seemed when first given if the austere character could have been known who would one day bear the name. Pettifer ultimately led to Potiphar with several variants on the way; it means the man with the iron foot. I recall that Dr 'Tubby' Clayton, founder of Toc H., liked to think that the Pettifers were descended from the Roman centurions who settled down as veterans in Roman London, and whose descendants, he considered, had lived on there right through the Saxon invasions.

Greathead and Broadhead are other characteristic names. Firebrace is derived, according to etymologists, from *bras de fer* or iron arm, meaning a very tough man, the French equivalent of Strongitharm. The name of Quartermain, rendered famous by Rider Haggard, means possibly iron fisted, or agile, since its literal meaning is impossible

Some of these names may have been bestowed for any but the reason given in the name, as it appears at first sight. Proud may have been a description for a shrinking creature, who could not speak up for himself, while the various forms of Strong or Strang may have been bestowed for anything except Herculean proportions. Shanks and Foot, Cruickshank, Foljambe bring us close to the type of unkind nickname. Foljambe, in particular, means a silly or useless leg—that is, a crippled one. 'Old cripple foot' was

89

probably the manner in which our more forthright and brutal ancestors referred to some poor fellow whose leg had been injured seriously. Swift may have referred to the man's speed of foot or his ability to make a quick get-away. Lightfoot, or Golightly, have a meaning which is akin, and Kingsley's Martin Lightfoot is a good case in point, although his was no surname. Ambler would refer to a man's gait; so, too, would Trotter. Proudfoot is hardly a nickname of joy, or love. Crooks is connected with Cruickshank. The numerous varieties of 'bottom', such as Ramsbotham, Winterbottom, Longbottom, do not refer to the lower part of the body, but to the variety of bottom or vale which was so important in an agricultural community.

Despite the large variety of surnames now in use, even larger must have been the number which fell out of use. Straight and direct were the christenings of our forbears. We find in the middle ages names such as Crypling, Handless, Onehand, Head, Neck, Mouth, Blind, Daft, Mutter and Stutter. It is fortunate that many of these names have not survived, at least for the peace of mind of the owners, who found it just as hard to shake them off, as schoolboys do who have had a nickname given to them.

A name like Blanchflower may have been encomiastic in the case of a woman, but decidedly derogatory with a man, implying perhaps that he was not up to manly standards. Lillywhite is a case of bestowal for reasons of complexion. There are many such names. Bell comes from the French, meaning fair, and thus was helped by its recipients to a good lease of life. Fairchild needs no particular thought and is a rare instance of a kindly nickname. Complexion has given many names to the English nomenclature. Blake comes from black and was caused by a swarthy complexion. White is obvious. If anyone doubts the fact of the bestowal of nicknames, he has only to think of the Chalky Whites, Nobby Clarks, Tinker Bells, and the rest of the tomfoolery which is the product not of schoolboys, but often of mature human beings.

White, Black, Red (in the forms of Read and Reid), but no yellow or purple. Green, as noted above, comes usually from the place of residence.

Not only the parts of the body have been laid under contribution, but the manner of walking, the demeanour and gait have given us names. Boff or Leboff comes from the French for bullock, meaning a great lump of a man who shambled along.

Boggs, or Boggers, can refer to a person who was apt to bluster or bragg.

The nickname, once given and hard to shake off in a small rural community, was passed down in the family, and over the generations the descendants acquired very different characteristics from those which their predecessors had possessed. This accounts for the complete contrast between the names as borne now and their meaning when first given, so that someone whose ancestor was renowned for Samson-like strength may well be puny himself. A well-known Irish family of the old ascendancy bears the name of Pennefather. This means a miser or close-fisted, and it is curious that an opprobrious nickname like this should have been retained. Stark is borne by many people today who have little in common with those medieval knights who were described as stark to their mortal foes, or like William the Conqueror, whom the writer of the *Anglo-Saxon Chronicle* describes as a stark man. Stark meant fierce or savage. Proudfoot is one of the expressive names given by our ancestors from the twelfth century onwards. Proud and pride are other nicknames; so, too, are Proudlove and Proudman. True-love gives us another picture, perhaps of someone whose love proved unavailing and who continued faithful to the end. They could not have omitted to beget children, however, or the name would not have continued.

For a very long time it has been the custom among various races to give characters to animals, such as the lion, the ox, the wolf and the lamb. These characters are usually derived from the observed behaviour of the animals and hence the bestowal of such names on human beings as nicknames. Fox is such a one; so is Wolf or Wulf; Brock is only another name for a badger. Roe, Ram, Cock are common. Lyon is the form usually given to lion. Hare and Stag are obvious. Beaver or Bever; Coney or Cony; Martin (may be sometimes from the Christian name or sometimes from the animal, the marten); Otter; Bull or Colt—all these are nicknames derived from animals and from their supposed characteristics. Some of these animal-derived names are of not very pleasant nature, as in Hogg or in Bore, Boar, Boor or Bor. Wolf in Latin is *lupus*, which was a Christian name in early Norman England. Lupus gave rise to Lovell, that one-time stock name for heroes of romance. Doe, Catt or Katt, and Hound all tell their tale.

Birds have contributed many surnames to our language. Bird

itself is very common. Falcon, Kyte, Jay, Peacock, Rooke, Parrott, Nightingale are all names familiar enough. They were bestowed upon some ancestor of the present bearer, because of the likeness between the man and the bird whose habits had become proverbial. Eagle, Sparrow, Goldfinch, Chaffinch, Pigeon, Dove, Drake, Woodcock, Partridge are all examples of names from the feathered creatures.

The number of nicknames is considerable, though it is unwise to assume that names which look like nicknames are really such. Sheepshanks is a case of a nickname, but many similar nams may, be derived from quite different origins. Duck, Turtle and Seoat are further examples of names from birds. From fish comte Pike Dolphin, Herring, Tench, Chubb, Lamprey and Spratt.

From general sources we may cite Welcome, Smallman, Quickman, Drinkwater, Whale, Cayser or Keyser,* Seafowl, Thickness, Toogood, Smart, Penny, Sad (meaning steadfast) and Sturdy. The fact is that large quantities of nicknames do occur in our older records, such as Sweatinbed, which have perished. It is no wonder that the bulk of the coarse or cruel nicknames of medieval times should have gone out of fashion, for who would want to own them? Their disappearance proves that the nickname origin of surnames is rightly relegated to the last place in the history of the subject. It would be much more natural for a person to shake off a surname which he disliked or resented, especially as such a name would be a reflection not only on himself but on his father or forbear.

* i.e. Kaiser (Caesar), a name from a play.

VII. Welsh Names

Every country needs genealogy to explain its history, just as the genealogy of every country requires its history to be understood if the genealogical studies are to be soundly based. In no country in western Europe, not excepting even Ireland, is genealogy so much needed as in Wales, in order to explain the history of the country and especially the history of its surnames.

Wales (Cymry is the name given to it by the inhabitants) is a name derived from the invading Saxons, who called those whom they dispossessed the foreigners or *weallas*. Whatever the truth of the matter, whether the Welsh are the remnants of the Britons, or whether the Britons managed to survive and live on, accepting the English language but filling the thin ranks of the invaders with their own abounding life, certain it is that the Roman Province of Britain disappeared, and its place was taken by the new country which came to be called England. The Welsh of the west—of Strathclyde, of Cornwall, and Wales itself—were hemmed in and cut off by the growth of the kingdoms of the Heptarchy. They had their own language, of the Celtic family (for want of a better term), distinct from the English; they had for a long time their own religion, for they refused or were said to have refused to preach the Gospel to the English; they had also a tribal form of organisation which, though similar in many ways to that of the English, was destined to live on long after the English tribes had grown into a nation.

This tribal organisation is the root of understanding of Welsh surnames. The old jokes based on the number of names in a Welshman's pedigree were simply bad examples of a worse habit, that of laughing about foreigners and their ways. Rees, ap Morgan, ap Evan, ap Caradoc, ap Bleddin, ap Griffith was not a surname in the English sense at all, but a string of genealogical facts, a rudimentary pedigree. The Welshman in reciting these six names had with him the account of himself and his family for a hundred and fifty years. He knew whence he came, and his exact genealogy was a rebuke to those whose genealogical knowledge was confined to a vague account of grandad.

The insistence on genealogy in Wales sprang partly from pride of race and partly from a mundane but necessary consideration. The practice of 'gavelkind' prevailed in Welsh law. This practice was the rule in Kent at one time, but otherwise had disappeared, or never prevailed, in England. Gavelkind meant the division of the family property among the sons of the deceased. It was this practice which weakened Wales, financially and economically, for it was impossible for the large numbers of gentlefolk to live well if in each generation they had to be content with a division of their estate; politically, too, for the same principle held sway, so that when a great Welsh king like Rhodri Mawr (*circa* 900) had succeeded in uniting all Wales, he yet allowed it to be divided again at his death, when his sons took it in equal portions. This habit or custom made Wales weaker than she need have been in the face of England. The consequence was that in due course Wales was conquered by England and has never regained her independence.

William the Conqueror purposely allowed his knights access to Wales, with the idea that their energies might be absorbed in conquering the Welsh and so give him less trouble in England. But the Norman Conquest of Wales was limited to the south. The north of Wales remained free until it was conquered by Edward I in 1282–84. Edward did, however, leave the Welsh their own laws, and contented himself with parcelling the country into twelve shires on the lines of the English administration. Wales remained under its own law—and gavelkind was part of the law. Because of the need for every man to be able to prove his identity and his right to his land, the Welshman carried his pedigree with him in his mind and on his lips; hence there was no need for surnames.

When a Welsh dynasty succeeded to the English throne, it might have been thought that the Welsh would regain a great measure of their freedom. Henry VII was very much a Welshman, and named his elder son Arthur, in honour of the old British King, Arthur of the Round Table. The son who succeeded him, Henry VIII, though himself half a Welshman, did more to bring Wales under English influence than ever did Edward I. For in 1542 Henry VIII put through Parliament the Act which united England and Wales. With the passing of this Act, English law prevailed in Wales, and one of the consequences was that surnames began to be assumed. For if the English lawyers refused to recognise Welsh law and customs, they also looked for the surnames with which they were familiar in England.

To the Welshman this meant one thing, that he had to conform to English ways and to take a surname. He did so by taking the name nearest to him, that of his father. Thus Evan became Evans, the son of Evan, John became Jones, the son of John. Griffiths was the son of Griffith, Williams was the son of William and so on. Hence the noblest families of the principality bear names which are common. Jones, Williams, Evans are so numerous as to be bywords for commonness, but they are simply patronymics which we have met elsewhere as the simplest form of surnames.

It is worthwhile to try to understand the meaning of these Welsh names, which are often the surnames of families whose histories go back to ages before the English conquest of England. They are full of romance and sometimes their traditions were in existence a millennium ago. This is the case with the Philipps family (the sons of Philip), which claims descent from Vortigern of Britain, that king of Kent who invited Hengist and Horsa into England. Further back still they claim descent from one Maximus, who in the fourth century rebelled against his liege lord, the Roman Emperor and made himself for a time the ruler of Britain. The true pedigree of this family—true, that is, as far as documents go— begins in 1089 with Cadifor ap Colwyn (Cadifor the son of Colwyn). Thus the accepted pedigree of the family, now that of the Viscount St Davids, is nearly nine hundred years old, and the tradition that they were of much more ancient stock was current in the tenth century. The surname of Philipps does not come into use in the family until the early sixteenth century. Then we have a clear picture of the growth of the surname, in three generations. Philip ap Evan has a son, Meredith ap Evan, whose son is named in the old Welsh fashion, Philip ap Meredith. The next generation is that of Sir Thomas Philipps, the last name being merely a translation into English of Thomas ap Philip, son of Philip.

Another interesting instance is that of Williams Wynn, the surname of a family of baronets, whose ancestry goes back in traced lines into the eleventh century. Then the first named ancestor of the Williamses is named Cadrod Harold, which means Cadrod the Handsome. His son was Idhon ap Cadrod. Some three hundred years later the name of the family is given as Williams. This may be a translation made later on of the earlier entries in the pedigree. At least the names are given as Evan Williams, whose son is William Williams. In the sixteenth century the name had definitely become Williams, for we have a clergyman and doctor of divinity, the Rev. Hugh Williams, whose son is the first baronet, Sir William Williams, created as such in 1688.

With the Wynn part of the surname we are able to trace in greater detail the process by which the surname of Wynn was attained. The first baronet of this line was one of the first crop of that curious rank of hereditary non-nobility, in 1611, when James I brought into being the order of baronets to enable the settlement of the six northern counties of Ireland to proceed. The name Wynn (Wynne), for the benefit of the numerous persons who own that name, is derived from an Old English word, *wine*, meaning a friend.

On the subject of the ancestry of the Wynns, *Burke's Peerage* waxes more than ordinarily eloquent (and this despite the fact that the Welsh pedigrees in that volume were subjected to a fierce and searching criticism as part of the post-war revision). It starts the pedigree of the Wynns thus: 'To the House of Gwydir, now represented maternally in one of its branches by the Williams Wynns of Wynnstay, must be conceded the first rank in Cambrian genealogy. This eminent family deduces male descent through their immediate ancestor, Rhodri, Lord of Anglesey, younger son of Owen Gwynedd, Prince of North Wales, from Anarawd, King of North Wales, eldest son of Rhodri Mawr, King of Wales. He succeeded in 843 his father, Mervyn Vrych, King of Powys, and by inheritance and marriage acquired the kingdoms of North Wales and South Wales. He married Angharad, sister and heiress of Gwgan ap Meuric, Lord of Cardigan, and had issue, Anarawd ap Rhodri Mawr,' etc., etc. After this excellent commencement to a family history, we pass through succession after succession of Christian names with ap in between, until we reach the sixteenth century when the surname Wynn, in conformity with English custom was adopted.

The family of Trevor, now represented in the peerage by Lord Trevor, whose surname is Hill Trevor, derive their ancestry from one whose existence has been seriously disputed by genealogists.

This may sound what is commonly termed 'Irish', because it is impossible to descend from a person who never existed outside the realms of myth. It could mean, however, that the eponymous person, from whom a tribe is named, never did exist, but was a mythical being. The name Trevor could then have come into existence because it was thought that the family did in fact descend from him; whereas in fact they merely assumed the name, through this wrong belief.

The name Trevor is indeed that of a place, a village in Carnarvonshire and another in Denbighshire. Tre in Cymric or Welsh is a house or a village. The eponym in question was one Tudor Trevor, who is described in various manuscripts as lord of Hereford, Bromfield, Chirk, the two Maelors, and Oswestry in Shropshire. He is not mentioned in any document until some three hundred and fifty years after his death and therefore an editor need not be a genealogical purist to feel that he can hardly start a pedigree with his name, and then leave a gap of about three hundred years before passing to the next named person in the pedigree. At any rate the surname Trevor, derived from the place if not from the person, is not taken until the Tudor period. The great families of Wales were no doubt the first to feel the pressure of English opinion which decreed their assumption of surnames. Tudor, by the way, or Tuder, is supposed to mean an under-tenant, and while this is certainly illuminating as to the origins of the famous Tudor dynasty, it also explains the fairly common dispersion of this surname, since under-tenants are not likely to have been a small class of persons.

To illustrate yet more the manner in which Welsh names have originated, it should be pointed out that the family of Lloyd-Davis of Whittington (in the *Landed Gentry*) also derive their pedigree from Tudor Trevor, so it is obvious that surnames are a late invention in Welsh. It is not until the later sixteenth century that this line of Tudor Trevor's descendants took the name of Davis. William ap David (hence the name Davis, or son of David) was inducted Protestant Rector of St Peter's, Worcester, in 1571, and his son was the first to bear the name Davis.

The name Lloyd is from the Welsh *llwyd*, or grey, a reference to colour as in the English surname Grey or Gray. Many Welsh surnames are thus Christian names which have become patronymics. Morgan has the meaning dweller by the sea shore, which would easily be conferred on a sea-dweller. Owen is used in the medieval romances in the form Owain. It is supposed to have a relationship with the name Eugenius—i.e. of noble origin. This is quite possible for two reasons. First, because the Welsh, until they became an industrial people, were much attached to genealogy and to placing a high value on noble birth. Secondly in the construction of pedigrees, in ancient Wales as in ancient Ireland, several elements were worked in together. There were the tribal pedigrees, then those of the Roman provincial worthies (like Maximus mentioned above), plus the ancient gods and heroes of the Celtic race, and finally, after the conversion to Christianity, the names of Scriptural and Old Testament notables. Thus the pedigrees of many old Welsh families in their medieval form are found linked with the genealogies of the Old and even of the New Testament. We shall find the same thing with the renowned Milesian pedigrees among the Irish in Chapter 9. These various sources have given to the Welsh many names—Christian names, that is, which have contributed towards the form of their surnames.

David comes, of course, from the Hebrew, meaning beloved. It was adopted in Wales on a vast scale probably because of the name of the patron saint of Wales, St David. Griffin (and Griffith), in Welsh, Gruffyd, was the name of several Welsh princes and is said to be from the Latin Rufus (or red), again being a reference to complexion or hair colour. Evan is the Welsh translation of the common John. Caradoc is common in the older pedigrees, and is of the same root as the Latinised form Caractacus.

Llewellyn is a name which causes disputes among etymologists, some saying that it comes from a word meaning 'like a lion', others that it is a form of the name Leoline. It has come into English, translated into the name Lewis, which is otherwise derived from France, and is supposed there to have had the meaning of 'loud battle', of which it can only be observed that it must have long since lost this meaning for parents in choosing their child's name. Ivor is another Welsh name, the origins of which cannot be exactly determined.

The use of the name David would perhaps lead to the question why more Biblical names were not used in Wales and thus brought into the surname category. The answer to this question is the same in England as in Wales. During the medieval period only a comparatively few Biblical names were in use as font names. Names such as Peter or Thomas or John were, of course, very common;

but when an Old Testament name is used, as with David or Samson, it will mean that the name was that of a saint, and the use of the name is derived from veneration for the saint, and not from an imitation of the name in the Bible. So much is this the case that a pedigree, which includes in the medieval period Christian names such as Joshua or Solomon, is almost certainly fictitious, since such Old Testament names were not used in the middle ages.

Many surnames come from the name of Samson, a Welsh bishop who went from Wales to Brittany, where he founded a monastery. His name, being used as a common Christian name in medieval times, became in due course a surname, and is found now as Sampson, Samson, Samsin, Sansom and other variants. The original name of the strong man of *Judges* meant 'like the sun'.

With the Reformation, however, the pattern of Christian names changed, and this led in Wales to the appearance of a number of surnames such as Jeremiah. The reason for this was the rendering of the Bible into the vernacular on a scale which could reach a very large number of persons. During the middle ages there was a large number of translations of the Bible, or at least of separate books of the Bible, into English, but owing to the slow process of copying by hand, they did not get across to as many of the people as the printed version of the sixteenth century. Yet many of the names of Biblical characters, like Noah or Adam or Isaiah, must have been familiar to the most ignorant from the Mystery Plays, or from the stained glass windows in the churches.

Inevitably in the composition of Welsh surnames the 'ap' must have been slurred over so as to form another name. Thus we have Prichard from ap Richard; also in the form Prichards. Prodgers is from ap Roger. Pumphrey, also Pomfrey, is from ap Humphrey. Bevan is from ap Evan. Pugh is from ap Hugh. Bevin, strange to relate, has nothing to do with this type of metamorphosis, but is from an old French form, meaning 'wine drinker'—in other words the opposite of Drinkwater.

The Welsh name Madoc (the name of the celebrated prince who was credited with the discovery of America before Columbus) is thought by some to be connected with the word for fire, and has certainly caused numerous surnames. Maddocks, Maddock and Maddox will occur to all, plus Mattuck, Mattock, etc.

A few names from England or from Anglo-Norman sources spread into Wales and were made into surnames. Roberts is a Welsh surname, coming from Robert, a name introduced into England from France. Howel is a well-known Welsh name, often used now as a Christian name. It comes from an old Breton source and may have got into Wales through some forgotten intercourse of the Bretons with their kinsfolk, the Welsh of Wales. During the troubles of the English Conquest, a number of Britons crossed over into Brittany and settled there. There was probably a flow back from Brittany in less disturbed times.

Dr Reaney gives an example of the change of Welsh surnames in the nineteenth century, which shows to what a late date the surnames were fluid. Thus a William Roberts was the son of a Robert Williams.

Much merriment has been caused in England and among the Scots over the names of the Welsh. Sir Walter Scott in *Ivanhoe* makes the jester Wamba sing of the widow who was wooed by three men—the knight of Tynedale, a gentleman of Wales, and a yeoman of Kent. The yeoman wins her hand, but not before Scott has had a dig at the Welshmans' lineage.

> *Sir David ap Morgan ap Griffith ap Hugh*
> *Ap Tudor ap Rhice, quoth his roundelay;*
> *She said that one widow for so many was too few,*
> *And she bade the Welshman wend his way.*

Here we have again the rather feeble joke about the plenitude of surnames in Wales, whereas, of course, we have only the joining of names of forefathers. Rees (as Rhice is more normally spelt) has given birth to the surname Price, from ap Rice or ap Rees. It is also the root of Rhys, Reace, Reece and Reese.

The Welsh, like the English, bestowed nicknames on people. Thus a man from England or who had been educated there was apt to be called Sais, a Saxon, or as the Highlanders say a Sassenach —and hence the name Sayce or Seys.

Vaughan is a Welsh name of widespread use among the greater families of the principality. It means 'small' or 'little' in the original language. Meredith is said to come from the same source as Morgan, meaning the sea; it began as a Christian name. Morris is derived from the French Maurice, which may mean swarthy or Moorish, so that Morris may be a nickname. Herbert means literally 'a bright army' and is from old German, having been adopted into Welsh. Powell is ap Howell, another example of slurring.

The name of one of the greatest Welshmen of our time is that of George, which has now in peerage annals become hyphenated to Lloyd-George. It may seem curious that a Christian name, which was brought into England from the Crusades, should have become a Welsh surname. George, the name of England's patron saint, who displaced from that position the previous holder, St Edward the Confessor, slowly came into use in England. In fact, but for the German princes who bore the name as Kings of England, it would never have caught on as it has done. It is now a very common Christian name in England and a surname in Wales. In England it is also found as St George, surname of a distinguished family of very ancient origin, who brought the name from France in the early Norman or Angevin period.

The practical disadvantages of Welsh nomenclature were well brought out by George Borrow in his book, *Celtic Bards, Chiefs and Kings*. He points out how hard it is to achieve fame if one's name is David Williams or William Jones. What a handicap, he says, to a poet!

VIII. Scottish Surnames

In dealing with surnames north of the Tweed, we need to remember that Scotland, more even than England, is an amalgam of races who have gradually intermingled, though not entirely. In early Scotland, that is in the three or four centuries before 850, when Kenneth MacAlpine became recognised as the King of all Scotland, there were five different kingdoms or realms. The Gaels or Scots who spoke Gaelic were in the west of Scotland; in the east and north-east were the Picts; the Vikings or Norsemen held the western islands; in Galloway, in the south-west, there was a kingdom of the Britons, and the south and east along what are now the borders and as far up as Edinburgh was a kingdom of the Angles, who formed part of the Heptarchical kingdom of Northumbria.

In 850 there was the fusion of Picts and Scots under a single crown. In 1266 the Hebrides or western Isles were ceded to the Crown of Scotland from Norway. It was not until the end of the fifteenth century that the Orkneys and Shetlands became part of Scotland.

Surnames were just as slow in developing in Scotland as in England and owed their rise in the northern kingdom to the same cause as in England, namely the Normans. The fusion of the five little kingdoms mentioned above was slow, and the standards of life were low; the influence which counted for most in Scotland came from England. At first, after the Norman Conquest, it was refugee Englishmen who went to Scotland. It was an English princess named Margaret who married, as his second wife, Malcolm III, whose nickname was Ceannmor, or Canmore, meaning Great or Big Head. This Margaret was the sister of Edgar the Atheling, the unhappy prince who was the rival to William the Conqueror for a period of about a month, but who afterwards took service with William; then finding that he was gaining nothing by servitude, fled to Scotland. While he stayed at the Scottish court under the protection of Malcolm Canmore, his sister was married to the Scottish king. She proved to be a great benefactor of the Scots, and was canonised as St Margaret. Queensferry is named after her. She brought with her many Englishmen, who felt that they could not stay in their native land with the Norman oppressors. Among these was one Liulf, Sheriff of the Northumbrians, who held lands at Swinton in Berwickshire from the Scottish Crown. His descendants gradually took their surnames from the land which they held, at Swinton. The great family of Swinton has continued in this tenure for over eight hundred years.

Swinton is but one example of the development of the Scottish surnames from places which were held by the respective families. In Scotland even to this day a man may be known simply by the name of his property. In the annals of the modern landed gentry of Scotland, there are many instances of the use of a territorial title by which the person is known. Thus we have Macpherson of Dalchully, known as Dalchully; or Cluny Macpherson. Numerous examples will be found by anyone who turns over the pages of *Burke's Landed Gentry*. Probably surnames derived from places form a larger element among the Scots than in England.

If at first many Englishmen fled to Scotland or sought refuge there, they were soon followed by Normans, who were scions of the Norman nobility established in England. These offshoots, like Barclay, found that they could not get sufficient advancement in England, and that as younger sons they must seek their fortunes elsewhere. In Scotland they were welcomed by the sons of Malcolm Canmore. The English names borne by some of these sons attest the influence of the English Queen Margaret. Among her children were Edward, Edmund, Ethelred and Edgar. One of her daughters was Edith, otherwise Matilda, who married Henry I of England and thus brought the old Saxon royal blood into the succession of the English throne.

Barclay was a younger branch of the Berkeleys, who were settled at Berkeley Castle, Gloucestershire. The Drummonds, who hold the earldom of Perth, are said by immemorial tradition to have come from Hungary with the father of Edgar the Atheling when he was recalled from exile to succeed Edward the Confessor. Drummond is a place name, being a variant of Drymen. It is also said that several other noble houses were derived from Hungary, by persons who came from that country in the train of the Atheling, and who afterwards settled down in Scotland. According to Hector Boece, one of the oldest Scottish chroniclers, Lindsay, Wallace, Lovell, Ramsay, Preston, Sandiland, Bisset, Soullis, Maxwell, Wardlaw, Gifford and Crichton were among those who came to Scotland with the Atheling and the future Queen Margaret.

The youngest son of Malcolm Canmore was David, known by his name of the Saint, because he bestowed large territories on monks and other ecclesiastics. He was termed 'a sair saint for the Crown', because his benefactions alienated large tracts of land from the royal domains. It is probable that he did this because he thought that the monks were likely to prove better cultivators than his own turbulent feudal chiefs. He certainly did consider that the newcomers from England would be better administrators than the fierce warriors who composed the court in the reign of his father.

Lindsay is variously derived from a place in France or, as seems much more likely, from Lindsay in Lincolnshire, an origin which exactly agrees with the supposed English stem of the family. If Wallace did actually come into Scotland with the Atheling, then in all probability his name does derive from Wallais, or Welshman, and the original ancestor may have been a Welshman in the train of one of the Norman settlers in Scotland. On the other hand, the name could come from one of the Strathclyde Britons, whose kingdom was among the five which composed the original Scotland. Lovell, a name which, as we have seen, was much used by romancers in the eighteenth and nineteenth centuries, comes from *lupus* or *lupellus*, a little wolf. The Lovells were seated in Somerset, and a branch emigrated to Berwickshire. The name is old French or Norman in origin.

Ramsay, the surname of the great Scottish house of the Earls of Dalhousie, is derived from the place Ramsey in Huntingdonshire. The name Ramsey, according to the great Swedish scholar, Eilert Ekwall, means wild garlic island. Preston is or was a local Scottish name of a place, now more often described as Craigmillar in Midlothian. It could, if the English origin is agreed, have come from Preston in England. Sandilands is from the place of that name in Clydesdale. The Sandilands were among the vassals of the great house of Douglas. No surname is of greater honour or grandeur in Scotland than that of Douglas, not even that of the royal house of Stuart; in fact often in the turbulent history of the Scots, the Douglas, Black or Red, had the upperhand over the Crown. Douglas is a place name, being derived from the principal lands of the family in Lanarkshire. The name means 'the black water.' Home is also a territorial name, the spelling of which has varied, some members of the family spelling the name Hume, as it is pronounced. David Hume, the historian and philosopher, used this spelling, but his brother spelt his name Home. The historian claimed that he had to spell as pronounced in self-defence because the daft English could not pronounce his name properly when spelt Home.

Bisset is definitely claimed as of Norman English origin, at least as regards the family, for the name is old French for 'rock dove'. Maxwell is from an English source, for the first of the line was granted a salmon pool on the Tweed, known as Maxwheel, this being from Maccus's Wiel, the Maccus being the name of the first recorded lord. Wardlaw, derived from a place or places in Scotland, and meaning the guard kept over the hill, is a fairly common name. Gifford is derived from the old French nickname of a fat, jolly person. The family of Gifford or Giffard settled in England at the Norman Conquest, and a branch came to Scotland. Crichton comes from the barony of Crichton in Midlothian.

Thus there are numerous Scottish names which are taken from place names. The widespread use of some of these, however, especially such as Maxwell, leads to consideration of a very important point in Scottish genealogy. I have already remarked on a similar matter in thinking of English names. Not all Howards can be members of the great house of Howard. Nor can all Maxwells be derived from the original person mentioned above. How do these names come to be in general use? Answers are various for England, but among the Scots I think the explanation is to be found in an understanding of the clan system. The clan is found in Scotland not only in the Highlands, but also on the borders.

Does anyone really believe that all Macphersons, all MacMillans, all Mackintoshes, etc. are related to one another? There may be such a belief, but the facts do not bear it out. The clan system is really a grouping around a central family of persons, who for various reasons want to gain the protection of that family's name. It happened in times past that there was a very great need for this. As we look over the records of the clans, we find many examples of what were known as broken men, that is impoverished or outlawed men, coming under the protection of the chief of some clan which was able to look after them. In this way many persons, who had no blood connection with the original head family of the clan, came to be incorporated and united with it. As far as genealogy is concerned, the head of the clan, the eponymous as he is called, is traceable for some hundreds of years. From his line spring the various branches which are genuinely connected with him. Then outside these well-defined limits come the horde of people collectively known as the Macphersons, MacFarlanes, MacVities, etc.

If one asks one of these people how far he can trace his ancestry, the answer will show quite clearly the artificial nature of most clanship. He will be able to trace his ancestry for three or four generations, like most people who have not taken the trouble to go into the matter. For the rest, the MacMillan or MacPherson, etc. takes a vicarious pride in the exploits of his clan. The clan for the majority of those who bear the name is an artificial thing. It does, however, enable the average Scot to be proud of an ancestry which he has not proved and which in most cases would be unprovable.

Take as an example the family of Maclaine of Lochbuie, more often spelt as Maclean. Here we have the case of an ancient family going back in its ancestry to the thirteenth century. Mac of course means 'son of' and in this family's history the great man was one Gillean. The name was originally spelt as MacGillean, the son of Gillean. Gillean was noted as the wielder of the famous battleaxe still used by his descendants in their crest. The branches of this great family are shown in the pages of both *Burke's Peerage* and of *Burke's Landed Gentry*, and they are carefully connected. But what of the numerous Macleans, Maclanes or Maclaines whom one meets in everyday life? Are they clansmen true? Well, in the growth of modern clan associations, they can be roped in, no doubt, just as a Sassenach pure and simple can be obtained (I was enrolled as a member of the clan Hay!) by adoption. But in most cases the bearer of the Highland names are not blood members of the particular clan. There is a good reason for this, because, as I said above, many persons came into the chief's protection. How clans broke up and went under is a matter of clan history. In Sir Walter Scott's novel, *The Fair Maid of Perth*, we see how a powerful association of clans underwent defeat in battle and never flourished thereafter. For such masterless men in feudal ages there would be only one course, and that would be to seek the protection of some powerful lord. Hence the assumption of the surnames of famous chiefs, by persons who had no blood connection with them. Hence, too, the septs which are found connected with most clans.

There is one clan, which for the past two hundred years at least can claim purity of blood. This is the clan MacGregor, and the story is so illustrative of clan history that it is worth telling. The MacGregors claimed descent from Gyric, the third son of King Alpin, who came to the throne in 787. The name was Latinised into Gregorius, and although the pedigree cannot be proved from this point, it at least accounts for the name 'sons of Gregor'. This clan is the most unfortunate in the history of the clans. For a long time it lost land to the Campbells, and at last came into conflict with the royal power. This was at the very beginning of the seventeenth century when the Union of the Crowns of England and Scotland was about to be accomplished. Between 1602 and 1603 the clan was in conflict with the Colquhouns of Luss, who were given the royal commission. At the battle of Glenfruin, in 1603, the MacGregors defeated the Colquhouns with great loss. Among the victims are said to have been some students from Glasgow University, who had come to see the battle, and who committed the imprudence of ridiculing the chief's half brother, who was known from his hairy appearance as the Giant Mouseman. He butchered the laughing students. Apart from this outrage, the slain were so numerous that their wives and daughters went in procession to James VI of Scotland (soon to be James I of England), wearing their menfolk's shirts over their clothes to show the blood-stains. The King in horror gave orders that the MacGregors were to be outlawed and an Act of the Scots Parliament was passed by which for all time coming the name of MacGregor was to be done away with.

In consequence of this the MacGregors practically disappeared from the land. In fact they adopted the names of various clans, such as Campbell (the famous Rob Roy MacGregor was often known as Mr Campbell), Cunningham, Dougall, Grant, Murray, etc. The present head of the family is a baronet and his ancestor, the first baronet, was known for the earlier part of his life as Murray. The ban lasted for some hundred and fifty years. In 1661 it was lifted by King Charles II, in consideration of the fact that the clan had fought for Charles I under Montrose. It was reimposed in 1693 under William of Orange and was not finally removed until

1784. At that time 826 persons came forward to demonstrate that they were MacGregors and that the chief of the clan was John Murray of Lanrick, who became Sir John MacGregor, the first baronet. Now these 826 must have been people whose forbears had prided themselves on being MacGregors and who were consequently more likely to have had MacGregor blood. It may have been, of course, that before 1603 the clan had been much mixed, but if it had losts its lands, as indeed it had before that date, then the chief would not have been in a good position to offer protection to any. So it seems that the MacGregors are the purest in blood of the Highland clans.

When I wrote up this story of the battle with the Colquhouns, in a popular article, I was astonished to receive a letter from a lady, who thanked me for exposing her mother's family, who had been MacGregors. She said that she had always hated her maternal relatives, because of the cruelties inflicted on her by her mother, the marks of which she declared she bore to the time of writing. Now that she had read about Glenfruin, she understood what was the matter with the MacGregors. Such are the details which illuminate the possibly otherwise dull study of genealogy.

Thus in Scotland, we have large numbers of surnames derived from places and from paternal names. The whole range of Macs afford a large selection of the second class. We can merely glance at some of the multitudes of the Mac names. Macpherson means son of the parson, and this raises an interesting question. Was the original of the clan the bastard son of a priest who broke his vows, or was the parson, in this case, not in clerical orders at all, but a lay abbot or lay vicar? The legitimate genealogy of the MacPhersons makes them descend from Duncan, parson of Kingussie, in 1438.

The great rival of the Macphersons, the Macintoshes or Mackintoshes, take their name from the toschach, the leader or front man. They are thus the sons of the chief or prince. MacMillan means the son of the bald or tonsured one. This could refer to a lay abbot or simply be a nickname referring to a bald person.

MacKenzie is the son of Coinneach, referring as often happens with clan names to some hero of the remote past. MacLachlan is son of Lachlan. MacLeod is son of Leod, which in itself is interesting because it is derived from the Norse name Ljotr, 'ugly'. The Norse influence made itself felt in a number of ways. The Norsemen contributed more than one clan to the Highlands. The Gunns, for example, are of Norse origin and their name is a diminutive from Gunnar, a Norse personal name. Gunnar can mean battle in its original Norse.

It would be tedious to work right through the various forms of Mac and its combination. It must be obvious to the most superficial view that the use of this form of surname on a large scale has added very greatly to the store of Scottish names, while at the same time reducing the number of distinctive forms. It is possible for a work to be produced which gives all Scottish surnames, and such a book is George F. Black's *The Surnames of Scotland*. It is only necessary to grasp the general principle of the Mac names to be half way on the road to interpret them. It may be noted in parenthesis that the Highland clans and their chieftains cannot trace their ancestry to anything like the length of the Welsh tribes and the Irish chiefs. Few clans are traceable before the thirteenth century.

Consequently, the surnames of the Highlands are not very old. It is argued that surnames were introduced into Scotland by Malcolm Canmore, and this is supposed to have taken place before the influence of his Queen Margaret came into question. He married her in 1068 and the convocation at which the innovation of surnames was proposed was held at Forfar, Angus, in 1061. Among the surnames then adopted, according to the old chronicler, were Calder, Lockhart, Gordon, Seton, Galloway, Lauder, Meldrum, Shaw, Gargill, Rattray, Dundas, Cockburn, Mar and Abercromby, Menzies and Leslie.

Menzies—whose pronunciation of 'Mingies' has been abandoned in Australia, where the name is borne by their statesman, Sir Robert Menzies—is said to be of Norman origin, and to have been at one time De Mayners. Calder is a place name, in Caithness. Lockhart is said to be an old French personal name, as Lochard. Seton is supposed to be from a place called Sai in Normandy. Lauder is from the place of that name in Berwickshire. Shaw has an interesting story. There are two Shaws, one of the south, the other of the north, the southern Shaw being a territorial name, the northern Shaw a translation from a Gaelic form, on the lines of Sithech, son of the wolf. The Shaws are a sept of the Macphersons, and the founder of the line of the Shaw baronets in Ireland, to which Bernard Shaw belonged, was a Scottish soldier who had come into England in the seventeenth century and was present at the battle of the Boyne. Bernard Shaw apparently joined the Macpherson clan association.

Cockburn is one of those names, frequently found in both England and Scotland, where the spelling bears little relationship to the pronunciation. The name is of a place in the Merse in Berwickshire.

Mar is also territorial; so, too, is Leslie, also spelt Lesley and Lesslie. This Scottish surname suffered a strange fate in England in the later nineteenth century, becoming adopted as a Christian name for both boys and girls. Abercromby or Abercrombie comes from a parish of the name in Fife.

Clearly the number of place names in Scotland is very considerable. To find out their meaning it is necessary to study a good gazetteer, and then to get a work dealing with the particular area. This will usually contain an account of the meaning of the place name. In this way the inquirer, who usually has only his own surname in view, will be able to work out its meaning.

Many of the greatest names in Scottish history are first found in an article which to Scotsmen has usually seemed an instrument of degradation. This was the famous Ragman's Roll, so called because of the uneven edge presented by the seals of the signatories to the articles of homage to King Edward I. This was in 1296 when Edward toured Scotland and forced its nobles and great men to become his vassals. He had made himself accepted as Lord Paramount, and he disposed of the kingdom of Scotland to John Balliol, who did homage to him. Balliol or Baliol is derived incidentally from the name of a small place a few miles south of Abbeville in northern France. This is a feature of the greater Scottish names which we meet again and again—that is, they are derived from places in northern France or in England, because the first bearers of them were already persons of gentle caste before they came to Scotland. In other cases, as with the Swintons, the original family when it entered Scotland did not possess a surname, but took one from the lands which it acquired.

Before going into the categories of Scottish surnames which follow those of England, it is fascinating to reflect on some of those names which have made the glamour and romance of Scotland's history appeal to many who have no Scottish blood. Hay and Haig are from the same root word, though this has acquired different meanings. Haig comes from the old English haga or enclosure,

110

from the root, hag, meaning to enclose. Hay is deduced from haga, haia, or haie, a hedge. The Hays derive from La Haye, a place name in France. In Scotland the family acquired great possessions and a distinguished feudal position. They were Butlers to the King of Scots, and to this day the head of the family has the post of Hereditary High Constable of Scotland. They hold the earldom of Erroll, which can pass through the female line, the present head of the Hays being the Countess of Erroll. She is the twenty-third holder of the earldom of Erroll.

The name Haig was originally spelt in the old charters as Haga, and the first mention of them is in 1162. From 1412 they spelt the name as at present—Haig. It was the celebrated Thomas the Rhymer who made the prophecy that whatever happened there would be a Haig at Bemersyde, their principal seat (in Roxburgh-shire, near Melrose Abbey). Some say that this was falsified when the main line of the Haigs of Bemersyde sold the property, after twenty-eight of them had been lairds of Bemersyde, so that they appear now in *Burke's Landed Gentry* as 'formerly' of the old estate. But in 1921 the Bemersyde House and the fishings on the Tweed were purchased for Field Marshal Earl Haig by his country-men. Thus the Rhymer's prophecy can scarcely be said to have slipped, save by a few years.

No name in Scottish history can be more soul-stirring than that of Graham (the variants are Grahame and Graeme). There can be few persons, properly apprised of the story, who can read the in-scription in St Giles', Edinburgh, on the tomb of the gallant Marquess of Montrose, so foully done to death by the Covenan-ters, without being moved. The great Marquess put his fortune to the test, to win or lose it all, and went with great courage to a dreadful death. His cause triumphed despite all and to this day his place of sepulture is a centre of pilgrimage to all, Scots or foreigners, who love true gallantry. Graham comes from an Old English root—a word, graegham, which meant a 'grey home'. This was the name of the manor mentioned in Domesday Book, as the possession of the family in England. Whether they were English or Norman can be fairly got over by dubbing the Grahams Anglo-Norman. At any rate, it is a curious reflection that the name of some forgotten manor should have provided the name for one of the most widely spread of all families of Scottish gentry.

To turn from the most illustrious to the more humble type of surname, that of Gow, which has a considerable interest in view of our earlier remarks on the ubiquity of the English Smiths. In another form we shall meet the Smiths in Ireland. Gow in Scotland means a smith, a trade which was important among the various clans for the same reason as I have stated in the case of England— namely the exigencies of constant warfare. Gow is a surname associated with Perth and its burgesses. It is tempting to think in this connection of Harry Gow, the famous smith of Perth, who took part in the battle of the North Inch in 1396, when the two bodies of Highlanders fought out their quarrel in the royal presence. Mason (Masson) is another well-known name in Scotland, which has a trade origin, though, as often happens with such names, there is also a family of Master Masons to the Crown of Scotland. This name is derived from the French word of the same meaning— Maçon.

——Ritchie and Rickart are diminutives or pet forms of Richard. Rutherford and Ruthven are place names. Rhind (Rhynd or Rind) also comes from a small place, Rhynd in Perthshire; it is a name which has achieved great fame through the endowment of the Rhind lectures in archaeology by Alexander Henry Rhind.

Ogilvie or Ogilvy comes from the old barony of Ogilvie in Glamis, Angus. The Ogilvies and the Campbells were formerly much at feud, with the result that the Bonnie House of Airlie was set on fire by the Campbells, and revenged by the Ogilvies in the burning of Castle Campbell near Dollar, in Clackmannanshire.

Campbell is from a Gaelic word meaning wry or crooked mouth. This must refer to the characteristic of some early chief of the line, like the name Scrope mentioned under English surnames. No family in Scotland has achieved greater success or more hatred (probably the two things are naturally connected) than the Campbells. Almost all the clans dislike them, even to this day, but it is perhaps the necessary tribute paid to success, for after every conflict or upheaval in the Highlands the Campbells came out of the turmoil with more property. Certainly there is no greater family among the nobility of Scotland.

Cameron has the meaning also of deformity in a physical sense, meaning a crooked or hook nose. This applies to the Highland Camerons, but the lowland family take their name from places in the lowlands. It is strange that nicknames of this type, which are distinctly opprobrious, should have stuck to the remote descendants. Yet four great houses—Campbell, Cameron, Scrope and Giffard—are marked in this way.

The Cummings are the same family as the Comyns, other variants being Cummings, Cuming, Cumine and Cummine. They are supposed to have come from Comines, near Lille in France. An old chronicler gives another version of the name. One of the earliest members of the family could not speak any language but his own Norman French. Yet he was keeper of the king's bed-chamber, and when he would admit anyone, he learnt to say 'Come in'. Hence he was known as William Come-in or Cumyn. It is always possible that this type of explanation is correct. The Comyns are probably remembered most at the present time for the murder of one of them by Robert the Bruce in a church at the beginning of his troubles. Incidentally, in connection with this family, there is a clear example of the way in which persons not of the same blood came to have the same surname. Many people sought the protection of the powerful Cumming chief, and he for his part was willing to accept them, but insisted upon them being known as 'Cummings of the hen trough' (because of a sort of initiation which they underwent in the castle trough), while true Cummings were known as 'Cummings of the blue blood'. In this particular case we have an insight into the growth of a clan, com-posed of all sorts of heterogeneous elements.

Chisholm takes its name from a border barony. By a strange shifting of ground, some of the Chisholms made their way into the north of Scotland and there became a small clan. Similarly, the Frasers or Frazers from being Scottish chivalry came to be a High-land clan. Their name was originally de Frisel, and was then con-nected with the fraise or strawberry plant in their ancestral woods.

Charteris comes from Chartres in France. Chenye, Cheney, Cheine, etc. is said to be from Quesney in Normandy. There were Cheyneys in Buckinghamshire, and from this source the Scotttish family is derived. An interesting account of one family of Cheyne in Scotland is found under Cheyne-Macpherson of Dalchully in *Burke's Landed Gentry*.

A trade name with a ring of antiquity about it is that of Mercer. An old verse has it:

> *Sae sicker tis as onie thing on earth*
> *The Mercers aye are older than auld Perth.*

Certainly more than six hundred years have passed since the Mercers emerged from a history unchronicled in books, but to be older than Perth they would need a greater antiquity than one would normally assign to a family sprung from a trade—that of mercer or draper.

Scottish names, whatever their local peculiarities, fall into the same classes as in other countries. Thus there are many simple patronymics, of which Wilson, Stevenson and Robertson are examples. Yet again the practice of using the Christian name of the father as the surname of the son also developed, so that there are many cases—Alexander, Andrew, Dick and Edgar—as in England, and also instances of the more natural formation, where we have Adams or Andrews, as son of Andrew, etc.

Trade, occupation, or office names made themselves a place in Scotland as in England. Baillie is a case in point. Mason and Smith have already been mentioned. Wright appears in Scotland as Wrycht; slater or tyler as Sclater; others are Porter and Fisher or Fischair. The absorption with hunting gave many names such as Forester or Parker, Warrener or Woodward.

A feature of Scottish nomenclature deserves to be noted. I mentioned earlier that in some parts of England where a particular surname happened to be frequent, it was customary to distinguish the holders by their occupations, so that we had Butcher or Grocer or Lawyer Hall. This is sometimes called a system of to-names, and in many small places in Scotland, a wide use of this type of surname is made. Dr Black mentions several examples in small towns, where there would be, for example, 17 Nicols, 19 Wisemans, 26 Wests, 68 Watts, etc. In these cases the only way to distinguish them was to give them nicknames, as we should be inclinded to call them. These nicknames could conceivably stick to the individual concerned and become a true surname.

Scotland preserves many forms which have become extinct in England, for Scotland has clung to her past much more tenaciously than has England. In heraldry Scotland is a museum where one can expect to find all manner of habits and customs long extinct elsewhere. So, too, with surnames; the greater preponderance of surnames derived from places reflects the feudal spirit of the land and its adherence even now to its romantic past.

IX. Irish Surnames

In considering the subject of Irish surnames we have to deal with various matters which complicate the straightforward analysis of the theme. For one thing, Irish pedigrees of the great princely families go back further than anywhere else in western Europe, and this fact necessarily has a bearing on the subject of surnames, because many Irish names are patronymics—e.g. the O'Connor Don.

Then, as mentioned earlier in other connections, history has a great influence on the study of genealogy in any country. The Irish for many centuries endured the rule of foreigners. After suffering greatly from the Norse invasions, they were subjugated in the twelfth century and ruled by England for nearly eight hundred years. Not only was there this foreign rule, but in addition it entailed religious persecution, because the English overlords were for four centuries of that time Protestants and so at variance with the fifteen hundred years of religious tradition of Ireland. The Catholic majority of the population lived under harsh penal laws, especially after the time of William of Orange (1689). It often happened that a family found it better to change its name and to adopt an English or Scottish equivalent. This did actually happen and accounts for one of the difficulties of Irish genealogy, because the same family may appear at different times under different surnames.

A case taken from *Burke's Landed Gentry of Ireland* of 1958 has relevance. There is an entry—O'Gowan of Bellamont Forest—which is headed by the name of Major-General Eric Edward Dorman O'Gowan. Later at the end of the article are found the names of his younger brothers—namely Captain Dorman-Smith and the Rt. Hon. Sir Reginald Hugh Dorman-Smith. In order to explain this seeming contradiction we have to go back to the beginning of the lineage, where we learn that the O'Gowans are a branch of the Cruthnean Dal Araidi of counties Antrim and Down.

In the reign of the first Elizabeth, Hugh O'Gowan, the chief of the name in Down, was transplanted from Down to County Cavan for giving aid to the O'Neill; with the passage of centuries and the deepening of the penal legislation, some of the family changed their names from O'Gowan to Smith.

The descent of the family mentioned above is then traced from Henry Smyth of Ballymoney, Co. Down, to the present representative. Dorman is a form of Dearman, itself coming from the roots 'dear' and 'mann'. Dorman, like Dearman and Durman, can then mean either brave man or wild man (wild animal). Its addition to the family name of Smith is simply in accordance with the usual assumption of additional names and arms, registered in the heraldic offices—in this case, the old Ulster Office in Dublin. The resumption of the name O'Gowan by the present head of this line is a feature of modern Irish nomenclature found again and again— i.e. a return to the old Irish clan name which had been hidden during centuries of oppression.

There must have been many similar cases where an Irish name was submerged for two or three hundred years and then resumed when Irish nationalism had gained for Ireland its independence of England. At the same time it is clear that the habit of stating that an English or Scottish name has really been a translation of an Irish one must lend itself in many instances to a false assumption of Irish nationality. It is a well-known fact that many of those who led the Irish in their final struggle against the rule of England bore names which were English, or at least not recognisably Irish. Michael Collins does not seem to be of an extremely Irish cast. Yet in a famous and useful reference work I read: 'Collins. A well-known English name. In Ireland it is nearly always the anglicised form of O Coileain, which is also Cullane. This sept is of county Limerick.' Now with great respect it is submitted that there are considerations of value why the name Collins should have been that of a family of English descent. Clearly in Ireland and in England often the same cause would operate which would create surnames. These surnames, derived from places or from patronymics, or being nicknames or trade names, could run parallel, so to speak, and their use in the two countries would not necessarily mean that the appearance of an English name in Ireland would always be a translation into English of an Irish name.

There is a very old and undoubtedly true saying that *Hibernicis ipsis Hiberniores*—the settlers became more Irish than the Irish themselves. If this were not true, how did the settlers repeatedly sent out from England disappear? They must have been absorbed into the Irish nation and found under the rain-clouded skies of their new country a new national outlook. With respect it is also suggested that the history of the Irish race does not lend itself to the appearance of great administrators and managers from out of its native ranks. Those who helped so decisively to overthrow England's rule in Ireland, and so prepare the way for the ruin of the British Empire, were very often of English or Scottish descent. I observe that the authority whom I quoted above has, *sub nomine* de Valera, the simple note—A Spanish toponymic.

Consequently, while I fully agree that the tyranny of the Protestant ascendancy often made it essential for an Irish family to assume an English or Scottish name, this must not be pleaded in all cases as the explanation for the appearance of a non-Irish name in Ireland. Haugh is a word which means a low lying meadow on the banks of a stream and is a name found in county Clare. The fact that the present bearers of the name are typically Irish does not mean that they are Irish in their ancestral origins. They could well be descended from a Scots settler or even from one of Cromwell's Ironsides. Beatty would seem to most people a Scottish name, yet is now claimed in certain parts of Ireland as being the English equivalent of biadhtach, meaning public victualler. The name must have been brought into Ulster by the Scots who were sent there to colonise the country. At the same time there may have been Irish folk who decided to take the name in order to escape trouble with the ruling powers. There could thus be two streams of the name—one from Scotland and the other a translation of the Irish.

I think, therefore, that the subject of Irish surnames can be complicated by purely nationalistic causes—the desire, now that England is for ever gone, to show that the bearer of an English-seeming name is really as good an Irishman as the next man.

During the time when I was preparing to revise the *Landed Gentry of Ireland*, after the lapse of many years, I visited Ireland and had the opportunity of talking with many Irishmen of all sorts and classes. In the result, the new issue of this old work was brought out after a gap of forty-six years. In its pages can be found layer after layer of Irish families, from the earliest princely houses until we reach the latest emigrants to Ireland, who have gone there to seek the peace which now seems to have descended upon this centuries-troubled land.

I shall have occasion to refer to the *Landed Gentry of Ireland* for illustration of family names in many cases. First and foremost we have to consider the great Celtic families of Ireland—the O's and the Macs. These mean, of course, son of, as with the Welsh ap, the Norman Fitz and the Scottish Highland Mac. There are still many of these ancient families. We have O'Callaghan, O'Carroll (coming from Kerball, which means warlike champion); O'Connell, O'Conor Don (descended from Conor, King of Connaught in the tenth century, and surnamed Don to distinguish him from his kinsman O'Conor Roe); O'Doneven, O'Donnell, O'Donoghue, O'Donovan, O'Ferrall, O'Grady, O'Hara, O'Kelly, O'Mahony, O'Shee—all of which are surnames formed from the Christian name of a chieftain in the distant past, usually in the tenth century, which has been made into a surname by the process of prefixing 'O' before the name. In the case of these Irish tribes, the chief's name was quite early, often in the tenth century, formed into a surname for his family and his clan.

Irish pedigrees are, as stated above, the oldest in western Europe. The reason for this may be found in the rapid acceptance of Christianity at the preaching of St Patrick. There were Christians in Ireland before his coming, but their influence was slight. The Irish might have continued in their paganism for ages but for the mission of this truly apostolic man. Within a generation of St Patrick's coming, the country was virtually converted. Then with the Christian faith came letters and learning. Ireland gradually grew into a scholarly land, with many religious foundations, and during the early middle ages, usually called the Dark Ages, Ireland's beacon light of Christian learning spread its beams far and wide. They were extinguished by the senseless cruelties of the Vikings, who were unable to conquer the land, but were able to impede its further progress.

The advent of Christian letters and learning meant that the pedigrees of the great families, who ruled the four provinces of Ireland and who provided the Ard Righ or High King, were written down within a generation or two of St Patrick's time. Therefore there is no sound reason for refusing authenticity to the pedigrees of the greater families from about 400 A.D. An interesting example of such a pedigree is that of the Maelseachlainn, whose

118

name has been Scotticised into McLoughlin. He descends from Niall of the Nine Hostages, who was High King of Ireland and who lived about 400 A.D. This Niall is always considered to have died about 405 on the banks of the Garonne. Thus he would be living about thirty years before St Patrick's coming, and so there is good reason to accept him as a thoroughly historic personage and descent from him as a matter of proven record.

After the Os we may consider the Macs. It is commonly thought that 'Mc' is Irish and 'Mac' is Scottish. Apart from the fact that the Scots came from Ireland, there are several well-known Irish Macs. Some of the more famous are MacCarthy, Macnamara, Mac-Mahon, MacGuiness and also MacDermot. These again are personal names which have had attached to them the prefix Mac, son of.

The Irish succeeded in bringing the Vikings to a stop at the battle of Clontarf in 1014; thereafter, the Vikings occupied several seaports, including Dublin, but did not penetrate further inland. Ireland might have regained her former position as a centre of peaceful civilisation, but for the unfortunate gift of Ireland to the English King. This followed from a Bull of Pope Adrian IV, who was the only Englishman to become Pope. He gifted the islands of the west to the English king, Henry II. The latter, too busy to carry out the papal donation, allowed Strongbow, Earl of Pembroke, to colonise Ireland, until such time as he himself could spare a few weeks to visit the country. Ireland was nominally conquered, which meant that a part of the country round Dublin formed an English pale. The rest of the land owed allegiance to the English king and to the nobles whom he set over the country. These nobles soon became more Irish than the Irish. Among the names which they brought into the country are such as Burke, Costello, FitzGerald, Dillon, Nagle, Walsh, Sarsfield, Power, Roche, Purcell and Barry. These names have long since become Irish.

Burke, which is a common Irish name, is derived from de Burgh or de Burgo. No more chivalrous name could be imagined, yet it has become the name of masses of humble Irishmen. FitzGerald became the rallying point for Irish rebels against the English Crown. Power is treated among English surnames and means 'poor', surely a curious transformation. Purcell is a nickname, meaning little porker. The meaning of these importations into

Ireland has thus nothing specifically Irish about it, and can be treated as for English names.

During the middle ages Ireland was never really subdued. Only two English kings visited the country, Henry II and Richard II, unless we count an unfortunate sojourn there by King John when he was only a boy, and when he succeeded in upsetting the Irish chiefs by pulling their beards as they knelt in homage before him.

With the coming of the Tudor dynasty a great change set in. Not only were the Tudors determined sovereigns, who insisted on their dominions being in order, but also there was halfway through the period the added aggravation of a difference in religion. The Reformation never flourished in Ireland among the native population. This led to persecution of the Irish by the ruling power. In the course of the seventeenth century two attempts were made to crush the Irish completely and almost to exterminate them. The earlier of these was the clearance of the six counties of the northern province of Ulster and the replacement of the native inhabitants by settlers from Scotland and England. This led to the arrival in Ireland of many surnames from these two countries. One example is Shaw, the name of a family of baronets, one of whose scions was, as I have said, Bernard Shaw.

Then, with the failure of an Irish revolt, there came the Cromwellian conquest. This was a success from a military point of view, in that English rule was again a reality, but it was accompanied by an almost deliberate policy of driving out the natives from province after province. In this process multitudes must have died from starvation and malnutrition. These movements from the English side of St George's Channel led to the introduction of many names into Ireland which are still there and are certainly not Irish in their origin.

Looking through lists of surnames for Ireland, we have the following which are of non-Irish origin: Abbott, Adair, Adams, Agnew, Allen, Aiken, Baldwin, Barbour, Aylward, Aylmer, Beatty, Barrington, Barry, Bell, Bellew (derived so it said from *de bella aqua* and hailing from Yorkshire); Pyne (described by one of our authorities, as 'mainly but not entirely Protestant gentry'); Lynch, Lunn, Lacy (this is the surname of a great Norman house); de Courcy (another Norman family coming from Somerset).

In short, the story of Irish surnames is that of a people of great antiquity who began to use surnames earlier than most races in western Europe. From the tenth century surnames are found in Ireland, belonging to the princely races. There is a story that the great Brian Boru, the victor of Clontarf, decreed that surnames should be adopted, but this cannot be proved. Still, it was within the century in which Brian died (he was killed as he prayed in his tent after the battle of Clontarf by some Danes who were fleeing from the fight) that surnames appeared in Ireland. These were always those of the Os and Macs, and were, as explained, a build-up from personal names, used as patronymics.

Then come the centuries under English rule, when a steady stream of immigrants from England come in during the middle ages. Attempts were made to get Irish names changed into English equivalents or to prohibit the use of Irish names altogether. There were also strenuous efforts to stop English or other non-Irish settlers from taking Irish names.

With the sixteenth and seventeenth centuries we have an influx of English and Scottish names, which bring great quantities of non-Irish elements into the country. While it is true that in some cases the Irish people did take foreign names, which were the translation of their own names into English, this process must not be used to explain too many names. Today the fashion is to de-Anglicise the name, so as to appear truly Irish, but this, I think, is simply a fashion. Antiquarianism dictated by politics is a strange and heady mixture.

Consequently, the consideration of Irish names resolves itself into a study of two kinds: (i) those names which are truly native and where the meaning is buried in the intricacies of the Irish language, and (ii) names which are not of Irish origin, but come from Scotland or England. Their meaning will follow the principles set out in earlier chapters.

Much study is now being given to Irish history and many new facts have been discovered. Certain provisos have to be observed when dealing with Hibernian prejudices. One learns early in one's intercourse with the Irish not to refer to Erse, though this was a perfectly sound word to use at one time. Erse is considered not good form because it implies the language of rough peasants and bog-trotters. The study of Irish history has, of course, been much impeded by the fire (not caused by the hated English) which destroyed the Four Courts in 1922. This was part of a civil war waged between bands of partisans and the Government forces, the

Government being the new republican authority which followed upon the departure of the British. This terrible loss has caused a hiatus in most Irish pedigrees which is, to say the least, unfortunate. It has, however, stimulated many scholars and research workers to try to find evidence for genealogical work, which would replace the material lost in the fratricidal strife of 1922.

X. Miscellaneous

However learnedly an author may discourse on the subject of surnames, most people care little for the principles which he enunciates
and are interested only in their own name. Yet it is necessary to
have these principles, because without them the most egregious
mistakes may be made in judging the origin of a name. In my own
family I have heard my paternal surname described as Scandinavian (with which it has no connection whatever) and my mother's
surname—Beswetherick—put down as either Dutch or Nor-
wegian, whereas it is plain Cornish. These remarks were made by
well-educated people, but who had made no study of the principles
on which surnames are now studied. As mentioned before, and as
should be emphasised again, the best clue to the meaning of a
name is to trace its genealogy.

Jewish names are often marked out as though almost determined by nature, though in fact few Jewish names as such really
exist. Without attempting to emulate or surpass Dean Milman in
a small compass, it can be said that the history of the Jews does not
exemplify a strict regard for racial purity. In the early days of the
Old Testament we read of a mixed multitude which came up from
Egypt with the Israelites; in later days there were persons such as
the Gibeonites, who were of different race from the Israelites; and
in times outside the Old Testament narrative, we know that
tribes of non-Semitic origin mixed with the Jews, particularly in
the Caucasian region. Now that the state of Israel is established,
Jews from all parts of the world are joining in a community, and
showing by their various physical characteristics that they represent different racial strains. Israel is, in short, a community and a
religion, not a race as such.

This difference in racial strains is reflected in the use of surnames
which are national and not of Jewish racial origin. Perhaps Cohen,

which denotes a priest, is one of the few truly Jewish surnames. We often hear of names like Bernstein, which are supposed to be specifically Jewish, but which are merely of German origin. If we wish to judge of the real value of Jewish names, we have only to ask ourselves why in this country Harris, or Sinclair, or Lewis, or Montagu are judged to be Jewish names. They most certainly are not in their origin Jewish, but have been assumed by Jews who have come to Britain. Nor is Disraeli a Jewish name, but one taken in Italy; nor are Montagu (Norman in origin) or Harris (Scottish) or Lewis (Welsh) to be classed as of Jewish origin.

With the passage of Jews from country to country, they have usually endeavoured to take to themselves names of the country, so that they might attract less notice. A name like Eisenhower might just as well be dubbed as Jewish or German Jewish, merely because we are not familiar with it. The father of the author of the *Golden Treasury* changed his name from Cohen to Palgrave. There have been many more similar metamorphoses. The name Barnett is not in itself in any sense Jewish; it is derived in many cases from the place of the name in Hertfordshire or from land which has been cleared by burning. It is now favoured by Jews from Germany or other parts of Europe, who have settled in this country.

When thinking of people who have come to settle here, we are inevitably impelled to reflect upon the makings of the English nation. I have already commented on Defoe's unfortunate verses in which he wrote of a polygeneous origin for the English race. I have myself heard this verse declaimed by a Jewish lecturer as a proof that when the Jews join themselves (as they frequently do) to the British aristocracy, they are only imitating the conduct of streams of immigrants in the past. The thesis advanced by Defoe cannot be supported. It is much more in keeping with the known facts that the people of these islands are comparatively homogeneous. Even if we admit the divide between Celt and Saxon, we are forced to see that Saxon, Viking and Norman were all much of the same stock, and this stock has peopled the greater part of the British Isles and has contributed the bulk of its population.

After the Norman Conquest and a period of some hundred years during which the Normans were gradually mixing with the English (already including the Vikings), there grew up in this country an intense hostility to foreigners, which is by no means extinct even now. From time to time during the middle ages, various kings tried to introduce bodies of foreigners. The only king to reverse the process was Edward I, who turned the Jews out of England, until Cromwell reintroduced them (in 1655). But always the great magnates of the realm, supported by the bulk of the populace, tried to exclude or drive out the foreigners—from Poitou or Anjou, or Gascony, Lombardy or Flanders.

Small bodies of Flemings, or of other foreigners, did get into the land and left names behind them which have gradually or swiftly been mixed with the rest of English nomenclature. Fleming is, of course, an example which springs to everyone's mind, but there are many other legacies in the form of surnames from the small bodies of strangers who made their homes here through commercial activity. Brabazon shows an origin from Brabançon; Main or Mayne from Maine; Hanway may be from Hainault; Lubbock from Lubeck; Brittain from Brittany; Champaigne gives its own clue. Yet many of these may not denote an ancestor from these lands, but one who went to them to engage in commerce and who received a nickname in accordance with that fact.

In the sixteenth and seventeenth centuries many persons found their way here from Holland, and later from France. A number of notable families came over with William of Orange. The pages of the *Landed Gentry* and of the *Peerage* give us Vansittart; Vandervelde; Van Keppel, now plain Keppel; and Van Cutsem. There was a much larger influx of Huguenot names when a considerable section of Frenchmen and women sought refuge in England from the tyranny of Louis XIV. Phene, Olivier, Martell, Maunsell, Peers, Averell, Bouchier and Folet are cited as examples of names from France. In many cases the name may be the same as that of an old Norman stock, but the family now in existence is derived not from someone who came over with the Conqueror, but from one of a boatload of exiles from France in the seventeenth century. At first there were Huguenot communities in England, and areas where the French tongue was spoken and where men and women worshipped in Huguenot chapels. These have all passed away and although there is a Huguenot society, there is no separate Huguenot community. They have melted into the main stream of English life.

After the seventeenth century, with its arrivals of Dutchmen, Frenchmen and Jews, there was no great invasion of foreigners, until the present time, during and after the war of 1939–45.

125

Colonies of Poles, Czechs and continental Jews have now become to some extent integrated with the British people. True, at present it is easy to find cases where the Polish language is spoken except when in conversation with the natives, when a halting kind of English is produced. In process of time these people may mingle with the surrounding British population. If so they will almost certainly in many cases anglicise their surnames. In some instances the original Polish or Czech name has been changed already to a completely different English surname.

The latest arrivals in this country, the West Indian or other coloured immigrant, have no language other than English and usually bear English names. The name of Sir Learie Constantine, for one example, is that of a Norman family.

The Roll of Battle Abbey frequently comes up for consideration when dealing with the subject of surnames. I have mentioned it in Chapter 2, but in view of its importance I think a longer reference may be useful here. One is often told that a certain person's name is on the Roll of Battle Abbey. In one text book, which I studied when I was a student of English literature at London University, there was the statement that the name of Chaucer occurred on the Battle Abbey Roll. I do not think that this claim can be substantiated from any of the copies of the Roll, even supposing these copies to have any corroborative value. The surname of Chaucer is said to be derived from the trade of a maker of chausses, or clothing for the legs. It is very unlikely that a tradesman's name would occur upon a Roll purporting to give the names of the noble ruffians who conquered at Hastings.

The facts about the Roll are hard to come by, but such as they are, they follow a legendary drift. It is true that Battle Abbey was founded by William as a thank-offering for his victory. It is most probable that some sort of list was maintained by the monks of persons whose souls they were to pray for. These would be possibly those of the Normans who had perished in the battle, but more probably the names on the Roll would be of benefactors to the Abbey, and in course of centuries these names would have been understood as those of fighters in the battle of Hastings. It has been said that the list contained places where the monks could insert names of subsequent benefactors. This would be perfectly in accordance with the use of the Roll as a list of those who had given something to the Abbey. There may not have been any fraud on the part of the monks or the donors to the monastery. When the Dissolution of the Monasteries took place, the contents of most abbeys, unless they were of monetary value, were shamefully dispersed. The Roll is supposed to have been taken away by the family to whom the Abbey was granted by Henry VIII, but nothing certain is known about this.

Several so-called copies exist of the Roll. These are by Grafton, Holinshed, Stowe, Scriven, Fuller, Foxe and Leland; also by Sir William Dugdale. One writer on surnames, Mark Antony Lower, says of these copies: 'It is remarkable that although many, perhaps the majority, of the names occur in all the copies, others occur in one or two only; and the difference between the copies is such as to render all attempts at collation useless.'

If we take Leland's copy as being the best, which seems to be the considered opinion of most who have written on the subject, we find that he has some five hundred names in his list. He is supposed to have seen and transcribed the original. There seems to have been an attempt to arrange the names in such a manner that the last syllable of the second pair rhymes with that of the first, and to produce alliteration in the placing of the surnames (so says Lower), almost as though the old principles of alliterative Anglo-Saxon verse had prevailed.

Thus we have such pairs as:

Aumarill et Deyncourt	Camoys et Cameville
Bertrem et Buttencourt	Hautein et Hanville
Baird et Biford	Warenne et Wauncy
Bardolf et Basset	Chaunt et Chauncy
Deyville et Darcy	Loveyne et Lascy
Pygot et Percy	Graunson et Tracy
Gurney et Greilly	Mohaud et Mooun
Tregos et Trylly	Bigott et Brown

It is clear that many of these names are of Norman or French origin, and many of them have been so cited in earlier chapters. The inclusion of Brown would at first sight appear a mistake, unless it is a translation of Le Brun. Still, no authenticity ought to be accorded to this Roll as a record either of those who fought on the Norman side at Hastings or of those who were among the first Norman families to settle down in the grand distribution of English lands recorded in Domesday Book.

It was the view of such writers as Sir William Dugdale, William Camden and Sir Egerton Brydges that the Roll was interpolated by the monks who had made it and that it was in any event a compilation much later than the eleventh or twelfth century. The late Rev. S. Baring Gould, in his book *Family Names and their Story*, has a chapter on the Roll. He says: 'We cannot doubt that there was such a roll at Battle, but at first it was a roll containing only the names of the dead whose obits had to be observed, and who had to be prayed for by name. But in process of time other names were added, successively, as paid for.'

Several books have been written about the Roll, by Sir Bernard Burke, son of the founder of *Burke's Peerage*, by Planché in *The Conqueror and his Companions*, and by the late Duchess of Cleveland, in *The Battle Abbey Roll*, published in three volumes in 1889. On the last named, Baring Gould remarked: 'The book must have had considerable labour expended on it. But it is not critical. The Duchess takes Holinshed's list as a basis for work, one of the most adulterated of all copies, and she lays some stress on the almost worthless *Dives Roll* as she calls it—a list drawn up by M. Leopold Delisle for the purpose of glorifying the French Norman gentry and of no authority whatever.' None the less, copies of the Duchess's work command a high price, as indeed do almost all the works on surnames which have retained any reputation whatever.

To sum up, Leland's version actually reproduces gaps in the original Roll, which were left by the monks in order to include names of Companions of the Conqueror when people were willing to denote something to the Abbey. That an original Roll of some sort was kept at the Abbey there is no good reason to doubt; that it had any really authentic list of Companions of the Conqueror is wide open to disbelief. It was in all probability a list of benefactors of the Abbey kept by the monks, who had realised the sales value of alleging that the names of benefactors were on the Roll. It is also a witness to the fact that many surnames did come into this country from Normandy or France, where they were earlier in existence than in England.

The Falaise Roll is another compilation which was drawn up in time for the visit of a number of descendants of Normans to Falaise, the Conqueror's birth place, in 1931, when some 315 names were placed on a bronze tablet erected in the chapel of the château of Falaise on 21st June, 1931. This Roll purported to carry the names of some prominent Companions of the Conqueror, but although very careful work went into it, it was based upon Wace's poem, *Roman de Rou*, which many modern scholars consider to have been inaccurate. The lists of known persons, who were present in the Norman invasion, are short and do not convey much help to those who seek to find their surnames on the casualty list or roll call of the Norman army after the battle.

Since Domesday Book is referred to very often in connection with surnames, it may be as well to say something about it. All sorts of things are stated in different subjects as having been mentioned in the Domesday. One of the most favourite quotes is to say that such-and-such a tree is mentioned in the survey. No trees—that is no individual trees as distinct from woods—are mentioned in Domesday. As far as I know, no individual trees are referred to at all in Old English literature, except the Holy Rood in the poem of the *Rood* and the hoar apple tree near which Harold fixed the stand of his army, afterwards known as Battle, but then (before 14th October, 1066) nameless. Similarly, if anything which looks like a surname is found in Domesday Book we may be sure that it is unlikely to be a true surname, unless it is a Norman name brought from overseas.

The Great Survey, as Domesday was called, was a record of the land of England (leaving out the four northern counties of Northumberland, Cumberland, Westmorland and Durham) to enable the Conqueror to know what moneys he could expect to get in from his vassals, and also what was the military strength of his realm. Thus it was at once the census and Schedule A of the eleventh century. The object of the survey was in no sense to give pedigrees, and of these there is no specific mention. In addition, there is a gap in the records of taxation after Domesday Book (1086) until we begin to get the Rolls of the Pipe (so called because for convenience in handling the manuscripts were rolled round a tube or stick), in the reign of Henry I (1100–1135). It is thus often hard to know whether a person named in Domesday Book as a landholder was the father or uncle of some other man named two generations later as holding the same property. For this reason genealogists are very rightly sceptical of claims to descent from persons mentioned in Domesday Book.

Manx names and Cornish names present problems to the student of surnames akin to those that he encounters when dealing with

Welsh, Irish or Highland Scottish names. The Isle of Man was a Celtic territory, which was invaded by the Norsemen or Vikings in the ninth and tenth centuries, ending in their establishing their rule over the island. In 1266 the country was ceded by Norway to Scotland, but the Scots' claim lapsed and English rule was established in the Isle of Man. The Norse names, according to various authorities, have passed into Celtic forms with a heavy emphasis on the patronymic type—Mac or son of. A peculiarity of Manx names is that often the Mac has dropped off—thus Christian, a name of a landed gentry family in the Isle, a member of which was the famous Fletcher Christian of Pitcairn Island and the Mutiny on the Bounty. The name was originally Mac Crystyn or Mac Christene. McCowyn is son of Owen, which has become Cowen or Cowan. McGray is a corruption from Mac Cray, or son of the weaver. McCorkyll has become Corkhill or Curkell, a Norse name from Thorketill, which was given the Celtic form only to lose the distinctive Mac after many centuries.

Quin is a Celtic name which was Mac Quin or Mac Cuinn in Ireland (also O'Cuinn) and which was found, too, in Man. The famous name of Caine was McCann or McKane, meaning the son of Cathan.

Another portion of the Celtic fringe is Cornwall, where the spoken language of Cornish died out in the early 1800s and has now been revived by a few language enthusiasts. The well-known saying, 'By Pol, Tre, and Pen, you may know the Cornish men,' is properly expanded thus (in Camden, and to which I referred in Chapter 3):

> By Tre, Ros, Pol, Lan, Caer, and Pen,
> You may know the most Cornish men.

The meaning of these prefixes is: Tre, a village or house; Ros, a promontory or wood, Pol, a pool or small inlet; Lan, an enclosure or church; Caer, a fortress; Pen, a head.

One has only to consider the number of Cornish names which one meets in the peninsula to realise that this jingle can be only an introduction to the subject. L'Estrange Ewen, quoting from sources of Cornish names, gives the explanation of such well-known surnames as Biddick, which is derived from *vidn ick*, or the meadow place. It should be noted here that the name Biddick occurs in county Durham, where there are two places, North and South

Biddick. If the name is genuinely Cornish, and there seems no reason to doubt this, it shows that Celtic forms have survived in places here and there in areas which were over-swept by the English Conquest.

Body is said to mean 'the dwelling by the water' in the original Cornish; Bolitho is 'the great belly', which stands for 'the hill'; Borlase is 'the green summit'; Bullivant 'the head of the spring'. In this list of Cornish names is included the well-known Carver, which would seem well accounted for, from the Old English ceorfan, to cut or carve, but which is supposed to be Cornish from car veor, 'the great rock.' Killigrew is the 'crane grove'; Kimber 'the little valley'; Nankivel, 'the horse valley'; Nepean 'the little valley'; Pember 'the short head'; Pengelly 'the head of the grove'. Penman (name borne now most appropriately by an eminent journalist who has been President of the Institute of Journalists) is derived from pen maen, 'the head of the rock'.

It is interesting to note that the name Penn, so famous here and in the United States, can come from Old English penn or fold, or Old English penn, meaning hill, as above in Celtic. Here must be one of those words so dear to the historians of the Indo-European group of languages, which are common to very diverse tongues. Winter is derived, in Cornish, from gwyn dour or 'the white water'. Winter is, however, also an English name, a personal name (that of a companion of Hereward the Wake, who fell with him in his last conflict), or a nickname. Rosevear is 'the great valley.'

There are naturally many other Cornish names not necessarily derived from local places. Names such as Jennifer (from Guinevere), Jewell, Keverne, Pascoe, Jago are fairly common in Cornwall and are genealogical names—that is derived from a founder's name.

Cornwall was known as West Wales, and many of those who came from it to England in the middle ages were dubbed as Welshmen. This is a reminder of the fact that the British Isles were originally inhabited by Celtic peoples, who, however much mingled with earlier races, had much in common as regards language and names. Into this Celtic enclave came the invading Saxons or English, who forced their control upon most of the best parts of the island of Great Britain, and subdued it on the whole linguistically as well. The later Vikings and Normans were of the same stock as the English and were eventually absorbed by them.

They both left their mark upon the nomenclature of the country, the Vikings in particular in the North and East of England, but the predominance of surnames from places are of English origin. With the toughening of the English stock by the Norman administrators, the rest of the British Isles were invaded, and Ireland was conquered. The net result has been a great anglicising influence throughout the whole area, so that the present trend to de-Anglicise Irish names, which are of non-Irish origin, is a reaction against the former English linguistic ascendancy.

The Channel Islands are a small enclave, which has not formed part either of the old Celtic dominion or of the Saxon races' peculiar territories. The Islands represent part of the Old Duchy of Normandy, which was lost to the English Crown in 1204. The Islands were not taken by the French and the sovereignty over them was agreed to be English when the final settlement came with France in 1259. The title of Duke of Normandy had to be given up, and so it is quite incorrect to style the Queen Duchess of Normandy.

The language of the Channel Islands has continued to be Norman French and they have their own government subject to the Sovereign of Great Britain, but not under the Parliament of Westminster. Consequently, the surnames of the Channel Islanders are of French pattern. Some of them are derived from fiefs, which they have held for many centuries, such as De Sausmarez, de Havilland or De Carteret. Others are of the familar type, such as Le Blancq; Le Gros; Le Hardy; Le Jeune; Le Petit; Le Feu; or occupational names like Bolanger (baker) and Le Maceon (mason). Others are of local origin, such as de la Court or de Anneville.

While preparing this book, I happened to mention to a journalist that I was writing it, and this led to an intense interest in the subject of surnames both in the national press and on television. Hardly was one of my television appearances twenty-four hours old before I began to receive letters from people all over England whose curiosity led them to write to me about the meaning of their surnames. I give a selection of these, of varying types, as they illustrate better than any amount of discussion the classes of surnames which excite curiosity: Wrightson; Bradman; Highams; Hibbert; Pearse; Witcher; Critchfield; Skillern.

Wrightson means 'son of the wright', the latter coming from Old English meaning a carpenter or joiner. Bradman, which means 'broad man', is found as early as the thirteenth century. Highams is the son of one Hayman, who was so named because he lived by the haya or haga, the enclosure.

Hibbert shares its place with Ilbert, Hilbert, Hibbard, etc. and is from one of those ancient Old German roots, *hildeberht*, which means 'battle glorious'. It should be stressed that this does not mean that the present bearers of the name are descended from some V.C. type of the dark ages, but that the name was originally a Christian name and became a surname, having lost most of its meaning in the process.

Pearse is connected with Pierce, Piers, Pears, Persse, etc. and is derived, somewhat doubtfully, from different roots, probably being from a form of Peter, a very common name in the middle ages, and abbreviated or altered into Piers, as in Langland's famous *Piers Plowman*. Witcher or Whitcher is derived from an Old English word which meant a chest; hence the word can mean a maker of chests and would thus be an occupational name. Critchfield is a local name, though the particular locality has disappeared or lost its name, since it does not appear in any gazetteer.

Skillern presents various difficulties, not the least the fact that it is a rare name. I think that it must be derived from the squiller or scullion, meaning rather the person who had charge of the vessels of the scullery than an actual washer of dishes. In the form squiller or squylloure it is often found in medieval records.

XI. Sources and Suggestions for Further Reading

No one who writes on or studies surnames can proceed without the help of his predecessors in the subject, even if he is merely disagreeing with them. From time to time numerous works on surnames have appeared, but many of these have been of an ephemeral nature and only a small number of books are worth studying on this matter.

The reason for this, as I have attempted to bring out in this book, is that while many have assigned reasons for the meaning of surnames, until quite recently there was little systematic or scientific study of the subject. The first writer on surnames in England was William Camden, in his book, *Remains Concerning Britain*. This work is out of print, but copies can be seen in libraries or obtained in antiquarian booksellers. The edition which I use is that of 1870. This has a section on surnames and is preceded by other sections which deal with Christian names; it is followed by sections on allusions, rebus or name-devises and anagrams. The study of Christian names does have a considerable bearing on the meaning of patronymic surnames.

William Camden lived from 1551–1623 and was one of the most learned men of his period. He held the posts of Headmaster of Westminster and Clarenceux King of Arms and his work was part of the great study which he made based on his tours of England, which bore fruit in his famous *Britannia*. Much of his work on surnames has lasted to this day, but in some instances he relied on the uncritical acceptance of the legendary meaning of a name.

From Camden's time to that of Mark Antony Lower is a long period, for Lower's work on surnames was published in 1843, under the title of *English Surnames: Essays on Family Nomenclature*.

It bore on its title page an effigy of William Camden, as 'the Nourice of Antiquitie.' In fact, there was a very real connection between the two, for Lower was the next writer to Camden who contributed anything of value to the study. He did a great deal to divide the subject according to the correct manner by his chapters on Local Surnames, Names derived from Occupations and Pursuits, Names derived from Dignities, etc., from Personal and Mental Qualities, from Christian names, etc. He was not above the type of derivation for a surname which is illustrated in the story of Aire (Airedale) mentioned in Chapter 2. A somewhat similarly ridiculous origin was assigned to the name Osborne.

Before we become too critical of these absurdities in older writers, it is as well to remember that genealogy was still (in the early nineteenth century) a study given over to amateurs, who might or might not be gifted, but who lacked any scientific approach to the study of pedigrees. Both place names and family trees awaited a much more critical approach, which was to come in the second half of the century. Even an historian as erudite and rightly critical as Lord Macaulay swallowed without hesitation many legends and even myths in the field of genealogy, though he easily saw through the legendary background of ancient Roman history.

The whole subject of surnames was placed upon a sound foundation by the works of Canon Charles Wareing Bardsley, whose book *English Surnames: Their Sources and Significations*, was published in 1873, and his *Dictionary of English and Welsh Surnames* (posthumously) in 1901. The second edition of *English Surnames* appeared in 1875. It has continued to hold a high place in the literature of the subject. Most of the definitions of origin of names hold good to this day. Bardsley gave due credit to Lower's previous work, which he described as being the first of real importance in the field.

Useful, too, in its way was the famous little work of Richard Chenevix Trench, (1807–1886), Archbishop of Dublin, entitled *The Study of Words* (1851). This book had passed through twenty-five editions by 1896. It did not deal with surnames, but with the meaning of words, and necessarily had much to do with eliminating legends and popular though erroneous ideas. If words were studied in this manner, the influence must spread to the etymology of surnames. All this was in conjunction with

135

the study of old English language and literature, in which such learned works as Freeman's *Norman Conquest* had a considerable share.

With the present century we arrive at a much more realistic study of genealogy with writers such as John Horace Round and Oswald Barron, who blew away the fables which covered the truth about England's greatest families. Their work was followed in many directions, and eventually the great peerage works had to admit their criticisms. Few fables now command any appearance in print with regard to family origins. In addition we had the work of the English Place Names Society.

The great need for the subject of surnames was a dictionary and this has been to some large extent met by the work of Dr P. H. Reaney, whose *Dictionary of British Surnames*, first published in 1958, has gone through several impressions. It gives origins for some 15,000 names; many more if one counts in all the variants. Still, if one remembers that there are some 100,000 surnames in the British Isles, it is clear that even if we reckon 30,000 names to be dealt with in Dr Reaney's work, allowing for the variants which he gives under the principal names, there are still many thousands of names not satisfactorily accounted for.

Other books which can be mentioned include two books by C. L'Estrange Ewen. The larger work is *A History of Surnames of the British Isles*, which is described on its title page as a Concise Account of their Origin, Evolution, Etymology and Legal Status. This was published in 1931, and the author also produced a sort of abridgement of his large work (*A Guide to the Origins of British Surnames*, 1938, described by the author as an epitome which rested upon his compendious History). Ewen's book was immensely learned and he covered a huge range of comparisons in other languages beside English. Many of his theories went contrary to the studies which were in favour when he wrote. It is, of course, almost inevitable that in any learned study there should be controversy between those who have deeply studied the matter; nor is anyone likely to be disappointed in this respect in the study of surnames. Compare on this matter Dr Reaney's note about Ewen's account of the origin of the name of Shakespeare. None the less, Ewen's work has great value, though the theories may often seem suspect. For one thing, he was a genealogist and therefore had the correct approach to his subject. In addition, many names are explained in his book which cannot be found in other sources, not even in Reaney. He gives lists of Cornish and Manx names not easily come by except in learned pamphlets and papers hidden away in scholarly magazines.

A book which commands a high price in the second-hand book-sellers' catalogues is *Homes of Family Names in Great Britain*, by Henry Brougham Guppy, M.B.Edin., published by Harrisons of Pall Mall, London, 1890. I do not think that there was ever another edition, and this would help to account for the price at which copies now sell. It is an interesting book, not exactly dealing with the explanation of surnames in this country, but with their distribution. The method of study is to show how a surname can be found in a particular part, or how widely it is distributed. For instance, we have the following note about the surname Scott; 'Irregularly scattered over England. Though the Scotts are permanently established in the south coast counties, as in Devon and Kent, and, including the Scutts, in Dorset, their great home is in the counties on either side of the Scottish border, in Northumberland and Cumberland on the one side, and in the counties of Berwick, Rox-burgh and Dumfries on the other side, and they are also numerous in southern Scotland south of the Forth and Clyde.'

A great deal of erudition has been expended upon this name, without obtaining full results. Clearly, a man named Scott, who lived in England, would be likely to have been of Scottish origin, and the name Scott would cling to him from some scribe's list where Scott appeared to differentiate him from others who bore the same Christian name as himself. But how did so many come to be in the extreme south of England? Were they settled there so as to be unlikely to make a dash for their native land? It is an intriguing explanation. The mention of Scutt, too, brings up the origin of this name, which is taken to be from a French word meaning 'spy'. This has been changed into Scott, so it is said. There are many unexplained mysteries in surname etymology.

The study of Christian names is very important in dealing with surnames. The best book on the subject is *The Oxford Dictionary of English Christian Names*, compiled by E. G. Withycombe (1945). This deals with roughly a thousand Christian names. The meaning of many of these goes far to explain many surnames which are derived from them. There is also a much larger work, which gives at least a mention of some eight thousand Christian names—*History of Christian Names*, by Charlotte M. Yonge, published in two volumes in 1863.

Miss Yonge was the author of the well-known novel, *The Heir of Redclyffe*, *A Book of Golden Deeds*, etc. and many other books. She brought together a great amount of learning in her book on Christian names and laid the foundations of the study. Miss Withycombe gives high praise to the book in the preface to her own work, but adds: 'The etymological part of her book is today almost valueless, but it contains a mass of anecdotes and facts about the history of names, which are still of interest and value.'

The study of place names has received impetus from the labours of the English Place Name Society. Vast stores of information are available in the many volumes issued by the Society. In addition, there is the monumental work, *The Concise Oxford Dictionary of English Place Names*, by Eilert Ekwall, now in its fourth edition. This author, who died in 1964, was a Swede, who had been Professor of English at the University of Lund, in Sweden. He acquired a great and justly deserved reputation as an authority on English place names. His dictionary is a mine of information and should be studied by all who wish to know the origin of our place names, which so often form the basis of English surnames.

With regard to Norman names I have already mentioned *The Origins of Some Anglo-Norman Families*, by the late Lewis C. Loyd. This valuable work gives sound information on the subject of Norman families settled in England. For those who have armed themselves against Norman legends, I suggest the reading of a book published in 1874, called *The Norman People: And Their Existing Descendants in the British Dominions and the United States of America*. This work is anonymous and its etymologies are uncertain, since it takes as proof of Norman blood the Norman sounding or seeming names found in the London Directory or on the facia boards of shops in towns in the nineteenth century. It adds a few grains of information here and there, but its main interest is the almost pathological desire which it manifests to claim Norman ancestry for masses of the British and American public.

Before tackling the subject of Welsh, Scottish and Irish surnames, it would be as well to study the series of essays in the opening of the definitive edition of *Burke's Landed Gentry* (1952). These essays include an article on English pedigrees by myself; on Welsh pedigrees by Francis Jones; on the Landed Gentry of Scotland by

138

Sir Iain Moncreiffe; and on the Study of Genealogy in Ireland by Anthony Crofton. The object of these articles was to give the users of *Burke's Landed Gentry* a key to the treatment of the pedigrees of the four races of the British Isles shown in the volume. Considerable help would accrue to anyone studying the surnames of the four races if he or she should first read these articles.

With Scottish surnames we have a very fine work—Dr George F. Black's *The Surnames of Scotland, Their Origin, Meaning and History* (1962). This book, published by the New York Public Library, was the result of a lifetime's research. It mentions, only to explode, many legends, and while we may regret them, we are bound to be glad of the truth which has been so painstakingly worked out by Dr Black. If one wishes to see what an older generation of scholars made of Scottish surnames, one should consult the three volumes work of William Anderson, *The Antiquity of the Scottish Nation*. In the nineteenth century it was still possible to bring out such massive works, and whatever their defects as to modern criteria of scholarship, they still contain great quantities of information which would not nowadays be available.

On the Highland clans, consult the large revision by the Lord Lyon, Sir Thomas Innes of Learney, of the book by Frank Adam, *The Clans, Septs and Regiments of the Scottish Highlands*, first published in 1908. It will prove of great help to the student of the Highlands, who will be often surprised at the origin of the clans.

Also of service on the same subject is Robert Bain's *The Clans and Tartans of Scotland* (1938), enlarged and re-edited by Margaret O. MacDougall, the latest edition being 1960. Both this and Adam's book are beautifully illustrated with clan tartan pictures.

The renaissance of genealogical studies in Ireland has produced several works by Dr Edward MacLysaght, dealing with surnames and their origins. There is his *A Guide to Irish Surnames* (1964), mentioned in my chapter on Irish names. This book was preceded by the author's larger works, *Irish Families: Their Names, Arms and Origins* (1957), *More Irish Families* (1960), and a *Supplement to Irish Families* (1964). Behind these again, the reader may care to investigate further into Celtic history with Father P. Woulfe's *Irish Names and Surnames*.

The most valuable source for Irish genealogy is the *Landed Gentry of Ireland*, which in its 1958 edition contained probably a wider coverage of notable Irish families than could be found in the older editions (those of 1899, 1904, and 1912). Here again the volume was opened by a series of articles useful to the genealogist and to the student of surnames. These prefatory articles were: The Irish Genealogies, by Prof. David Greene, in which the nature of Hibernian pedigrees was carefully and sympathetically discussed; Irish Surnames, by Dr Edward MacLysaght; The Changing Picture of the Irish Landed Gentry, by Mark Bence-Jones; The Royal Peers of Ireland, by Philip M. Thomas; Irishmen in the British Military Service, by L. J. Garland; The Bench and Bar in Ireland, by V. T. H. Delany; and The Irish Genealogical Research Society, by Wallace Clare.

In this connection, the references which I have given to *Burke's Landed Gentry* and to *Burke's Peerage* are not without good reasons, for these two books contain thousands of pedigrees, there being not fewer than 2,400 in the *Peerage* and about 4,500 in the *Landed Gentry*. In many cases the origin of the surname is given or can easily be worked out, and these instances are a great help in studying surnames.

It may not be readily understood that there are indices of pedigrees, from which it is possible to know almost at once whether or not a name has much in the way of pedigree or family history behind it. There is the nineteenth century work, *The Genealogist's Guide to Printed Pedigrees*, by George W. Marshall, which appeared in 1879 and passed through several editions, bringing the inquirer in the end up to the early years of this century (1903). Taking the story on from there we have *A Genealogical Guide*, compiled by J. B. Whitmore, which is described as an index to British Pedigrees in continuation of Marshall's *Genealogist's Guide*. This was published in 1953, and unless a pedigree has existed only in manuscript carefully hidden away, it is sure to get a mention in one or other of these works. If they are used in conjunction with *Burke's General Armory of Coats of Arms*, the inquirer can usually lay the ghost of any alleged pedigree. Very useful, too, in dealing with claims of pre-Conquest descent is the work by William George Searle, *Anglo-Saxon Bishops, Kings and Nobles* (1899).

It is almost impossible to give a full list of the books which would be useful to the reader who is trying to work out surnames and wants to connect his genealogy so as to discover the first forebear who had his surname. The books listed above are a start and nothing else, for they are only the most outstanding or most useful books. If anyone wishes to go more deeply into the study of family history he would be well advised to consult the Society of Genealogists, whose address is 37, Harrington Gardens, London, S.W.7. Here in the rooms of the Society the inquirer will find a large collection of books dealing with all aspects of family history and he is sure to obtain clues as to research elsewhere, at the British Museum, for instance, or Public Record Office.

Index of Subjects

Index of Surnames
Mentioned in the Text

929.4
P

Pine, L   G   11/67
    The story of surnames.

Wilmington Public Library
Wilmington, N. C.

RULES

1. Books marked 7 days may be kept one week. Books marked 14 days, two weeks. The latter may be renewed, if more than 6 months old.

2. A fine of two cents a day will be charged on each book which is not returned according to the above rules. No book will be issued to any person having a fine of 25 cents or over.

3. A charge of ten cents will be made for mutilated plastic jackets. All injuries books beyond reasonable wear and all losses shall be made good to the satisfaction of the Librarian.

4. Each borrower is held responsible for all books drawn on his card and for all fines ac-ing on the same.